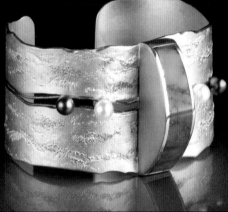

Jewelry Design Challenge

10 MATERIALS
30 ARTISTS
30 SPECTACULAR PROJECTS

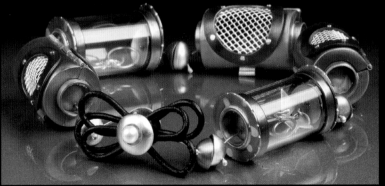

LINDA KOPP

LARK CRAFTS

A Division of Sterling Publishing Co., Inc.
New York / London

Senior Editor
Marthe Le Van

Editorial Assistance
Amanda Carestio

Art Director
Kathleen Holmes

Junior Designer
Carol Morse

Photography Director
Dana Irwin

Photographer
Stewart O'Shields

Illustrator
Orrin Lundgren

Cover Designer
Celia Naranjo

Library of Congress Cataloging-in-Publication Data

Kopp, Linda, 1960-
  Jewelry design challenge : 10 materials, 30 artists, 30 spectacular projects /
Linda Kopp. —1st ed.
    p. cm.
  Includes index.
  ISBN 978-1-60059-602-5 (pb-trade pbk. : alk. paper)
  1. Jewelry making. I. Title.
TT212.K68 2010
739.2—dc22
                                2009049875

10 9 8 7 6 5 4 3 2 1

First Edition

Published by Lark Books, A Division of Sterling Publishing Co., Inc.
387 Park Avenue South, New York, NY 10016

Text and Photography © 2010, Lark Books, A Division of Sterling Publishing Co., Inc.,
unless otherwise specified

Distributed in Canada by Sterling Publishing, c/o Canadian Manda Group,
165 Dufferin Street, Toronto, Ontario, Canada M6K 3H6

Distributed in the United Kingdom by GMC Distribution Services,
Castle Place, 166 High Street, Lewes, East Sussex, England BN7 1XU

Distributed in Australia by Capricorn Link (Australia) Pty Ltd.,
P.O. Box 704, Windsor, NSW 2756 Australia

The written instructions, photographs, designs, patterns, and projects in this volume
are intended for the personal use of the reader and may be reproduced for that purpose
only. Any other use, especially commercial use, is forbidden under law without written
permission of the copyright holder.

Every effort has been made to ensure that all the information in this book is accurate.
However, due to differing conditions, tools, and individual skills, the publisher cannot
be responsible for any injuries, losses, and other damages that may result from the use of
the information in this book.

If you have questions or comments about this book, please contact:
Lark Books
67 Broadway
Asheville, NC 28801
828-253-0467

Manufactured in China

ISBN 13: 978-1-60059-602-5

For information about custom editions, special sales, premium and corporate
purchases, please contact Sterling Special Sales Department at 800-805-5489
or specialsales@sterlingpub.com.

For information about desk and examination copies available to college and
university professors, requests must be submitted to academic@larkbooks.com.
Our complete policy can be found at www.larkbooks.com.

Contents

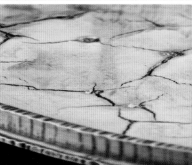

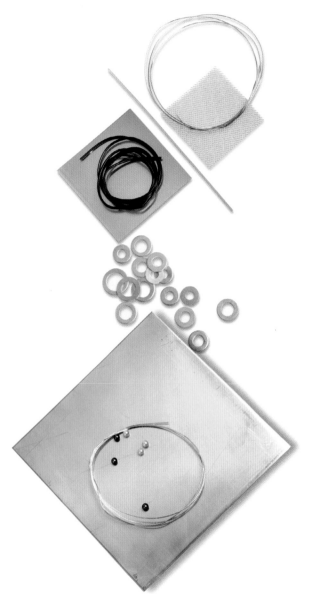

What If?

Curiosity. That's where this book started. What would happen if we asked a group of top jewelry designers to trade in their usual jewelry supplies—fine gold and precious gemstones—for basic materials like copper sheet and washers?

Our curiosity led us to action and this simple concept: we'd assemble a box of nine basic jewelry materials, send identical boxes to 30 artists, invite each person to add a wildcard element to the mix, and let the creativity take off.

Ten Supplies, 30 Approaches

And take off it did. To some, like Marcia Macdonald, the challenge seemed the perfect catalyst for renewed creativity. For others, it was a welcome reprieve from their normal, full-steam-ahead production mode. It became clear that, while we were quite literally inviting jewelers to participate in a design challenge, it was really an invitation to something more: a chance to explore, to innovate, to step out of the standard… or, in the words of participant Bob Ebendorf, to play.

We admit we were tempted to include some very unconventional elements in our box of materials—along the lines of watch parts, a bottle cap, and ball bearings—but we eventually settled on a set of basic ingredients that would be relatively inexpensive and accessible to anyone.

Material Icons

18-gauge sterling sheet, 3 inches (7.6 cm) square	18-gauge copper sheet, 6 inches (15.2 cm) square	1.6 mm sterling tubing, 6 inches (15.2 cm) long	Six 5mm black and white pearls (½ drilled)	15 copper washers, (5) ¼ inch, (4) ⁵⁄₁₆ inch, (3) ⅜ inch, (2) ⁷⁄₁₆ inch, (1) ½ inch (.6, .8, .95, 1.1, and 1.3 cm)	20-gauge sterling wire, 36 inches (91.4 cm) long	Medium fine silver mesh, 6 cm square	1.8mm round Greek leather cord, 36 inches (91.4 cm) long	20-gauge copper wire, 36 inches (91.4 cm) long

From Ordinary Elements Came Genius

As the challenge results began to trickle in, we were stunned, as much by their creativity and vast diversity as by their sheer beauty. It was hard to believe that the designs were made from the humble materials we sent. Varied technical approaches seamlessly incorporated personal style and aesthetics, all within the restraints of the assigned materials. And what a range of styles: from spirited, almost whimsical pieces to technical masterpieces, and everything in between.

The artists had different approaches to the materials. Some used every scrap—such as Thomas Mann who created as many pieces as possible with the supplies—and others used only one or two. And then of course there's the wildcard, which in some cases is quite wild. In many instances, the artists picked signature elements of their established working style: Rebecca Hannon's multi-colored laminate, Robert Dancik's faux bone, Candie Cooper's felt, Boris Bally's industrial metal, and Janette Schuster's tintypes. Others chose to forego the wildcard, taking a pared-down approach to the challenge.

Kinetics plays a prominent role in a handful of the works like Annie Chau's caged pearl ring (page 66) or Tod Pardon's sculptural pendant (page 94), while others include interchangeable parts—such as Joanna Gollberg's utterly versatile necklace featuring a reversible pendant that can hang vertically from either end or horizontally. Chihiro Makio's engineering marvel boggles the mind as it transforms from necklace to bracelet, to ring, brooch, and earrings.

Several artists took our basic materials and used them to create something with personal meaning. Kathy Frey's ring was created mid-move; hence it's many swirling parts. Marcia Macdonald's brooch (page 51)—made surprisingly with a lovely bit of harvested road paint—represents a return to creativity with a new perspective.

What you have here is an amazing account of the event in the form of the 30 resulting pieces and how-to instructions for each, plus a bit of the story of how each design came about. You're privy to the inner workings and techniques of artists who don't typically reveal their processes, along with insights into their approach to the challenge and images of their other works.

Join us on this amazing journey of creation and revelation.

How You Use this Book

With this book you get to see inside each artists' process and methods, with step-by-step insights into how they created their pieces and expert tips from the experts themselves. To get started, use the icons on page 4 to determine which materials each artist used in his or her design. These same icons will appear at the beginning of each project. If an icon is darkened, that means it was used in the creation of the piece. There are three tools kits used sporadically throughout the book (see right). The project instructions will state which tool kit/s will be needed to create the piece. Refer to the appropriate kit and gather the tools listed.

You can follow the how-to instructions for a project exactly or use these inspirational designs as a jumping off point for your own design. Perhaps you've fallen in love with Joanna Gollberg's washer chain (page 107), for example, but you're also inspired by Thomas Mann's pod forms (page 30): combine the two treatments into one totally different piece, creating your own unique response to the challenge. The combinations—and opportunities for fun—are truly endless. And here's a final added bonus: as high-end as these pieces appear, aside from some of the wildcard additions, the materials used to make each of the design challenge projects are affordable and can be easily purchased online from jewelry suppliers like Rio Grande.

Bench Tool Kit

Stainless-steel ruler with metric measurements

Scribe

Calipers

Dividers

Bench pin

Steel bench block

Anvil

Metal snips or shears

Jeweler's saw frame

Saw blades: 1/0, 2/0, and 3/0

Beeswax or lubricant for saw blades and drill bits

Needle files: barrette, half-round, round, square, and triangular

Bastard file

Pliers: round nose, flat nose, and needle nose

Chasing hammer

Forging hammer

Mallet: rawhide, wooden, or plastic

Mandrels

Dapping block and punches

Rolling mill

Center punch

Flexible shaft machine

Drill bits in assorted sizes

Wood block

Burrs

Separating discs

Sandpaper, 220 and 400 grit

Brass brush

Burnisher

Green kitchen scrub pad

Polishing machine and compounds

Polishing attachments for flexible shaft

Soldering Kit

Soldering torch

Striker

Heat-resistant soldering surfaces, such as charcoal blocks, firebricks, or ceramic plates

Flux

Flux brush or other applicator

Hard, medium, and easy solder

Snips for cutting wire solder

Small embroidery scissors for cutting sheet solder

Solder pick

Tweezers

Cross-locking tweezers with wooden handle

Copper tongs

Water for quenching

Pickle

Pickle warming pot

Safety Equipment

Safety glasses

Safety gloves

Hearing protection

Dusk mask and/or respirator

Fire extinguisher

Bally • Baran • Bigazzi • Chau • Coppelman • Cooper • Dancik • Davies • Ebendorf • Frey • Gollberg • Hannon • Hettmansperger • Hood • Karash • Lora • Lynch • Macdonald • Makio • Mann • McCreight • Miller-Gilliam • Pardon • Reed • Schuster • Schutz • Silva • True • Warg • Westermark • Bally • Baran • Bigazzi • Chau • Coppelman • Cooper • Dancik • Davies • Ebendorf • Frey • Gollberg • Hannon • Hettmansperger • Hood • Karash • Lora • Lynch • Macdonald • Makio • Mann • McCreight • Miller-Gilliam • Pardon • Reed • Schuster • Schutz • Silva • True • Warg • Westermark • Bally • Baran • Bigazzi • Chau • Coppelman • Cooper • Dancik • Davies • Ebendorf • Frey • Gollberg • Hannon • Hettmansperger • Hood • Karash • Lora

• Schutz • Silva • True • Warg • Westermark • Bally • Baran • Bigazzi • Chau • Coppelman • Cooper • Dancik • Davies • Ebendorf • Frey • Gollberg • Hannon • Hettmansperger • Hood • Karash • Lora • Lynch • Macdonald • Makio • Mann • McCreight • Miller-Gilliam • Pardon • Reed • Schuster • Schutz • Silva • True • Warg • Westermark •

Design Number I
Created by **Sydney Lynch**

each charm has character and singular detail...simple technique for marriage of metals...components work individually or grouped

Tools & Materials

Bench tool kit, page 6
Soldering kit, page 6
Tungsten welding rod soldering pick*
Satin finish wheel
Disk cutter
Checkering file
Coarse rubberized abrasive wheel
Liver of sulfur
Two-part epoxy, slow-drying

Wildcard

Sterling silver tubing,
3 mm outside diameter

Expert Tip: *I use a tungsten welding rod, sharpened at one end, as a soldering pick. It may qualify as my most useful tool. You can pick up a chip of solder by melting it onto the end of the pick, and then position it wherever you need to solder carefully.

Method

Making the "Stick" for Each Charm

1. Use a bench cutter or saw to cut strips of the sterling silver sheet that are approximately 2 mm wide. Turn the strips on edge on a steel bench block.

2. Using the flat end of a hammer, hammer the strips to slightly texture their edges. (The hammered edge of the strip will face front on the charm.) Cut the strips to the desired lengths with a clipper. File and smooth the cut ends with emery paper.

Preparing the Tubing Spacers & Bails

1. Saw out 3 mm lengths of the 3 mm silver tubing, as many as needed. Use 280-grit emery paper to smooth the cut ends.

Expert Tip: If you want a brushed finish, thread the small tubes on a piece of binding wire, twist a loop in both ends of the wire so the tubes won't fall off, and polish the tubes with a satin-finish wheel on a buffer.

From the Box

Charm 1: Small Leaf with Copper Accents

1. Cut a small piece of sterling silver sheet. Solder small bits of copper wire to the surface of the silver sheet with easy silver solder. Sandwich the piece inside folded paper, and run it through a rolling mill a couple of times until the copper wire is flattened and level with the silver sheet.

2. Draw a leaf shape on the sheet with a marker. Saw out the shape, and file its edges. Slightly dap the leaf on the backside using the round end of a hammer. Refile the edges, and smooth the leaf with emery paper.

3. Solder a hammered silver stick onto the back of the leaf. Solder a small silver tube to the back of the stick, a few millimeters below its top end.

Charms 2, 4, & 8

1. Use a bench cutter, shears, or a saw to cut small squares or rectangles out of the sterling silver and copper sheet. If desired, curve the metal pieces with a hammer against a stump or wooden block, or curve them with round-nose pliers. Smooth all edges with emery paper.

2. Try the following embellishment options:

Cut small lengths of thin sterling silver tubing. Solder the tubes on end to small pieces of copper or silver sheet with easy silver solder.

Melt tiny metal scraps with a torch to form balls. To make a pellet shape, place a ball on a bench block and smack it with the flat end of a hammer. Solder the ball or pellets onto the metal squares with easy solder.

Snip 5 to 6 mm of sterling silver wire. File one end flat, and solder it on end to the hammered stick. (You'll trim the wire to the proper length later, when attaching the pearl.)

3. Lay the small silver and copper shapes facedown on a soldering block. Solder them to the hammered sticks with easy solder. Solder a small silver tube to the back of each stick, a few millimeters below its top end.

Charms 3 & 10

1. Choose lengths for the hammered sticks. Use shears to cut the silver mesh into the desired shape.

2. For charm 3: Saw a copper washer in half, and file the cut edges flat. Texture the front surface of the washer with the narrow end of a hammer. Flow a snippet of hard solder onto the cut ends of the copper washer. Position the washer facedown on a soldering block. Position a hammered stick flush with the ends of the washer, and solder together.

3. For charm 10: Solder a small silver square to the hammered stick instead of the half washer.

4. For both charms: Position the mesh facedown on a soldering block along the edge of the hammered stick. Use snippets of easy solder to solder the elements together, heating the stick first and allowing the heat to conduct to the mesh.

5. For charm 10: To make a post for the pearl, solder a short length of sterling silver wire to the bottom end of the hammered stick.

6. For both charms: Cut several pieces of sterling silver wire, each approximately 6 mm long. Use a torch to melt one end of each wire into a ball. One at a time, insert the wires through the mesh in the same direction. Place the balled wire side of the mesh facedown on a soldering block. Pointing the torch flame sideways, ball the back end of the wires. Solder a silver tube bail to the back of each hammered stick.

Charm 5

1. To form the copper oval, sandwich a washer inside folded paper and roll it through a rolling mill. With a knife-edge file, create a texture of radiating lines across the front of the copper oval. Slightly dome the oval by dapping the back with a wooden punch and mallet.

"Some of the materials, especially the metal sheet, were like a blank canvas, while items like the pearls, washers, and the mesh, which I've never used before, would inform more specific design details."

2. Use a disk cutter to make a circle from the sterling silver sheet. Place the silver circle in a dapping block, and dap it with a steel punch.

3. Solder the copper oval and the silver dome to a hammered stick. Solder a small piece of sterling silver wire in the center of the silver dome to use as a pearl post. Solder a silver tube bail to the back of the hammered stick.

Charm 6

1. Use shears to cut out a leaf shape from the silver mesh. Cut a strip of the copper sheet that is 1.5 mm wide. Turn the strip on edge on a steel bench block. Using the flat end of a hammer, hammer the strip to slightly texture its edges. Slightly curve the hammered copper stick with your fingers. Cut the strip to the desired length, and finish its ends.

2. Place the copper stick facedown on a soldering block. Position the mesh leaf facedown on top of the stick. Pick solder these elements together with easy solder.

3. Make silver balled wires, and solder them into the mesh as described in step 6 of Charms 3 & 10. Solder a silver tube bail on the back of the copper stick. Use your fingers to shape the mesh and add some dimension.

Charm 7

1. Sandwich a large copper washer in folded paper. Roll the washer through the rolling mill once or twice to form an oval shape. Place the copper oval in a stump or wooden dapping block, and dome it with the rounded end of a ball peen hammer. Cut a slot in the top of the domed oval with a saw. Insert a hammered silver stick into the slot, and solder the pieces together from the back.

2. Make silver pellets (see step 2 of Charms 2, 4, & 8 for directions), and solder them to the front of the oval. Make a pearl post by soldering a sterling silver wire to the bottom end of the hammered silver stick. Solder a silver tube bail to the back of the stick.

Charm 9

1. Roll two different sizes of copper washers through the rolling mill to make two oval shapes. Draw a flower petal design around the perimeter of the larger copper oval, and saw out the design. File and smooth the cut edges. Lightly dap the copper flower with a wooden punch and mallet.

2. Flow easy solder on the top surface of the smaller copper washer. Solder the top surface of the small washer to the back of the copper

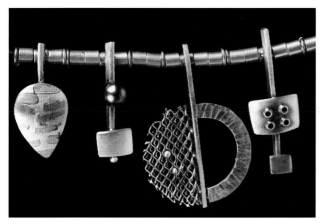

flower. Solder a hammered silver stick behind the top of the copper flower. Solder a wire peg for a pearl behind the bottom of the flower. Solder a silver tube bail to the back of the hammered silver stick.

Charm 11

1. Use a checkering file to texture the edges of two copper washers of the same size. Cut one of the washers in half with shears or a saw, and file the cut edges flat.

2. Flow snippets of easy solder onto the cut ends of the half-washer. Position the half-washer perpendicular to the full copper washer, and solder. Solder a hammered silver stick to the top of the full copper washer. Solder a tube bail to the back of the hammered silver stick.

Charm 12

1. Draw a leaf on the sterling silver sheet, and saw out the shape. File and smooth the cut edges with emery paper. Drill holes in the silver leaf with a bit that matches the copper wire. Cut lengths of the copper wire that are approximately 2 mm longer than the thickness of the sterling silver sheet. Lay the silver leaf face-down on a soldering block, and a few at a time, insert the copper wires into the drilled holes. Solder the copper wires in place with snippets of easy silver solder. Repeat this process until all drilled holes are filled with copper wire.

2. Clip off the ends of the copper wires, but don't file them yet. Using a wooden dapping punch and mallet, dap the leaf form from the back. File and sand the edges of the silver leaf.

3. Solder a hammered silver stick to the back of the silver leaf. Solder a tube bail to the back of the hammered silver stick. Use a wide, flat file to smooth off the ends of the copper wire on the front of the leaf, filing and sanding until you see the copper dots. Use a coarse rubberized abrasive wheel on a flex shaft to smooth

off the copper wire on the back of the leaf. Finish the front of the leaf with fine emery paper.

Charm 13

1. Punch a disk out of the copper sheet, and dome it with a steel punch and block. Texture the edges of the dome with a checkering file.

2. Solder a hammered silver stick to the back of the copper dome. Solder a wire peg for a pearl in the center of the front of the dome.

Finishing the Necklace

1. Select a small mandrel that has a similar diameter to the silver tubing. Wrap the copper wire around this mandrel, and make a large number of jump rings from the coil. Close each jump rings with needle-nose pliers. (I didn't want to see the silver solder on the jump rings, so I didn't solder them closed.)

2. If desired, immerse the finished charms in a liver of sulfur solution. Rinse and dry the charms, and then brush off most of the oxidation with a satin-finish wheel on a buffer. (You can also use a satin-finish attachment with a flexible shaft.)

3. Select two copper washers of the same size to use for the clasp. Saw narrow slots in the washers. Texture the washers with the narrow end of a hammer. Make two jump rings from the sterling silver wire. Using the edge of a file, notch each washer where you want to anchor a jump ring. Solder the jump rings, seam side down, to the notched edges of the washers.

4. Cut two 3 mm lengths of sterling silver tubing to use as end caps. Sand the ends of the tubing smooth with emery paper. Roll a small piece of the silver sheet through the rolling mill, thinning it to 24 gauge. Solder one end of each tube to the thinned silver sheet. Trim off the excess silver sheet, and file and sand the seams. Make two more sterling silver jump rings. Solder one jump ring to each end cap with the open seam facing up. Attach the washers to the end caps, and solder the jump rings closed. Finish the findings with a satin wheel.

5. Cut the leather cord to the desired length. (I used 17 inches [43.2 cm] of cord for an 18-inch [45.7 cm] necklace, including clasp.) Check the drill holes in the pearls against the lengths of the wire pearl posts, and adjust by trimming the posts and/or redrilling the pearls. Assemble the necklace, stringing the tube spacers, the jump ring spacers, and the charms. Use slow-drying, two-part epoxy to glue the end caps onto the leather cord and the pearls onto the posts. Let the epoxy cure overnight.

Insight

When the design challenge box arrived, it was a little like opening a Christmas gift—a mixture of anticipation, excitement, and a little anxiety. I let the materials sit out on my design table for a couple of weeks while I looked at them from time to time and began to let some ideas percolate. Some of the materials, especially the metal sheet, were like a blank canvas, while items like the pearls, washers, and the mesh, which I've never used before, would inform more specific design details. My best thinking time occurred while I swam laps and could clear my head of distractions.

I finally sat down and made detailed sketches for about six different pieces. Eventually there were a couple of finalists. I wanted to include as many of the materials as I could in the piece, and since it was slanted toward writing instructions for someone else to follow, I decided to make the necklace a kind of sampler. I have made many of what I call "charm" necklaces, so this would be a new twist on a design familiar to me. There were a few other designs I liked as much as the one I finally made, and it would have been fun to make two entirely different pieces for the challenge, then decide which one I preferred. Ultimately, I think the hardest part of the challenge was having to make a single choice when there were so many directions to choose from.

artist: Sydney Lynch

Created by **Jennaca Davies**

Design Number II

organic geometry...
modern take on classic
nautilus fold...perfect
nest for pearls

Tools & Materials

Bench tool kit, page 6
Soldering kit, page 6
Photocopied design template,
    page 127
Rubber cement
Draw plate or draw table
Draw tongs
Rotary tumbler
Two-part epoxy, quick dry

Wildcard

Sterling silver wire, 18 gauge

From the Box

Method

Constructing the Silver Spirals

1. Using the rolling mill, thin the sterling silver sheet to approximately 28 gauge. Adhere the photocopied template onto the silver sheet with rubber cement.

2. Cut out seven small circles and one large circle. Using a metal scribe, carefully mark the 16 interior sections of each circle. After peeling away the paper, you will see 16 clearly marked sections on each circle.

3. Using a jeweler's saw, cut along one of the marked lines on each circle until you reach the middle.

4. To prepare for bending the circles, score the metal with a square file along each scribed line of every circle. Score approximately 70 to 80 percent through the metal, enough that the circle folds nicely but does not break. Anneal each scored metal circle.

5. Hold one circle at one side of the cut line. One at a time, slightly bend each scored section until the circle spirals together. Repeat this step to bend all remaining circles.

Creating the Links for the Chain

1. Using a draw plate or draw table, thin the 20-gauge wire to 22 gauge. Create approximately 63 jump rings that are between 2 and 3 mm in diameter. Solder the seams of the jump rings closed.

2. Cut eight jump rings in half. You now have two half rings for each spiraled silver element. Solder two half jump-rings onto the back of the spirals, placing them four sections apart and near the pointed end. This placement helps to counterweight the spirals when they are sitting on the neck.

3. Cut eight pieces of the 18-gauge sterling silver wire, each 0.95 cm long. Cut 16 pieces of the 18-gauge wire, each 1.6 cm long. Solder one closed, 22-gauge jump ring to each end of all cut wires, making sure the rings face the same direction.

Joining & Finishing the Necklace

1. Connect the chain by sawing open the jump rings and linking the elements together. Repeat this order four times: small silver spiral, long link, short link, long link. Connect the large silver spiral to the last long link, then repeat this order three times: long link, short link, long link, small silver spiral. Complete the chain by adding one long link, one short link, and one long link after the last spiral. Solder all open jump rings closed.

2. Create a simple hook from the last link of the necklace that will fasten into the silver spiral piece at the back of the neck. This way, the closure remains fairly hidden when the piece is worn.

3. Solder a small length of wire to the center of each of the middle three spirals in the necklace. (The three pearls will be attached to these wires after all metalworking is complete.)

4. Tumble the necklace to work harden the metal and clean up any sharp edges or scratches on the piece.

5. Using the two-part epoxy, affix half-drilled pearls to the wires soldered inside the three middle silver spirals.

Insight

I was intrigued by the project from the start. The concept was unique and required me to approach my design methodologies a bit differently. Typically when I design a piece, I begin with a certain shape or form that I have created through model making. This project forced me to change my approach and begin my work with a set group of materials. It was challenging, but overall a good design exercise.

artist: Jennaca Davies

Design Number III

Created by **Boris Bally**

masterfully constructed frame…found object is elevated…interest on front and back in equal measure

Tools & Materials

Bench tool kit, page 6
Soldering kit, page 6
Silver tube clasp, handmade
  or commercial
Commercial silver pin hinge and tab
Stainless-steel wire for pin stem,
  1 mm
Machinist's square
Sharp graver
Matting brush for polishing lathe
  or sandblaster
Ball burr, 5 mm
Fine brush for cleaning/aligning
  pin hinge hole

Wildcard

Recycled aluminum license plate
(Pennsylvania)

From the Box

Method

1. On the silver sheet provided, measure and scribe parallel lines that are 6 mm apart. Cut out this strip with a jeweler's saw. Repeat this process to create a total of four strips. File all edges flat. Cut the strips to equal 2¼-inch (5.7 cm) lengths. File the strip ends to exact 90° angles.

2. Position the strip ends on edge to make a frame, and solder together with hard solder. Pickle, rinse, and dry the frame. File the solder seams, and square the edges of the frame.

3. Scribe a line all the way around the inside of the frame, 1.6 mm down from the edge.

Expert Tip: With a graver, create a small burr that will later hold the middle sheet in place during soldering.

---

4. Using the remainder of the silver sheet, cut a square that is slightly larger than the silver frame. Flatten the square on a steel block with a leather mallet. Once flat, file its edges slowly and cautiously until the flat sheet fits tightly inside the frame.

5. Solder the flat sheet inside the frame with medium solder. (I like to stick feed this from a solder wire, but you can lay down snippets.) Pickle, rinse, and dry. Clean up the seams with a sharp triangular file. Create a matte texture on the flat sheet with a matting brush.

6. Use calipers to measure an internal rectangle on the flat sheet. (In this project, the rectangle is 16 mm from the top, 9.5 mm from the bottom, and 6 mm from each side.) Drill

a pilot hole, and then saw out the interior rectangle. File and deburr the cut edges.

7. Stamp your signature, the date, a hallmark, and the metal purity on a scrap piece of silver sheet. Saw and file the scrap to create a nice rectangular (or any desired shape) "tag." Solder the tag to the back of the brooch.

Expert Tip: Using a small ball burr, remove a channel of metal around the perimeter of the back of the tag. Heat and flood this channel with medium solder. Pickle, rinse, and dry the tag. Plane the back of the tag flat on a piece of 220-grit sandpaper. Place the tag on the back of the brooch in the desired location. Flux and heat the metal. The solder will flow without moving the tag.

---

8. Attach the pin findings to the rear of the brooch with a small chip of easy solder. Important: Placement of the pin clasp is critical. The brooch will later be riveted, and ample room must be left for this connection. (In this project, the clasp is 7.9 mm below the edge of the frame.) Also, the pin stem must enter the clasp from the bottom. This orientation secures the brooch even if the clasp opens accidentally. Pickle, rinse, and dry.

9. Cut the license plate in any direction you want, and carefully file it to fit inside the front of the silver frame. The fit should be very tight to aid in holding it secure. Using a small drill, make a hole through both metal layers at the location where you wish to trap the pearl. (This hole will allow you to line up the indentations made in the next step.)

10. Place the license plate on a wooden stump. Using a 5 mm punch, create an indentation centered around the drilled hole. Repeat this process to indent the piece of silver.

Clean up the drilled holes with a round file, leaving enough of a "lip" to trap the pearl.

11. Cut and fit the mesh into the square frame. Cut a circle out of the mesh where the pearl will be housed, so the mesh doesn't interfere with the seating of the pearl. Test to make sure the entire assembly fits together nicely. Almost done!!

12. Finish the silver frame using 220-grit and then 320-grit emery paper. Buff only the outer edge of the frame to a high polish. Hint: Use a felt buff to keep the flat sides flat. Wash to remove all buffing grit.

13. Measure and mark a point near each corner of the brooch that is 4.7 mm inside each edge. Drill a 0.8 mm (18-gauge) hole at each marked point.

14. Straighten and then cut silver wire to length for four rivets. Trap the pearl in the indentation. Do a "once over," and make absolutely certain that everything is done and ready for the final connection.

15. Rivet each of the four wire rivets with a cross-peen hammer. (This is a difficult step. You may first want to spread and dress the rivets using a round, then flat, then hollow punch.) Beware of denting your beautiful brooch.

16. Fit the pin stem to the clasp so it's the correct length. Sharpen the stem, and rivet it into the hinge with the supplied wire. To complete the brooch, polish the silver with a yellow or red rouge medium.

Insight

I selected the license plate to offset the "newness" and polite frailty of the box materials. I HAD to add a little flavor, patina, and a BANG of color.

artist: Boris Bally

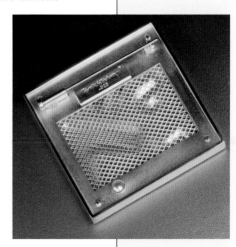

Design Number IV

Created by **Kathy Frey**

> "Ultimately, working on a project that isn't in my typical medium of wire got me to do more sketches in a series that I want to develop that is all about balance."

jewelry at play…washers
follow symbolic orbit…
whimsical and full of spirit

Tools & Materials

Ring-measuring tool
Cardboard
Bench tool kit, page 6
Soldering kit, page 6
Awl
Tube cutter
Liver of sulfur
Glue (optional)

Wildcard

None

From the Box

Method

Making the Ring Band

1. To make a template for the ring band, find the desired size on a ring-measuring tool and trace its inner circle onto cardboard. Use a circle template to trace the larger, outer diameter of the ring band. Cut out the cardboard template, try it on, and modify the shape as desired. (For a more comfortable fit between fingers, I modified my band to be slightly more oval and narrower at the sides.)

2. Transfer the template onto the sterling silver sheet by tracing it with a scribe. Cut out the band with a jeweler's saw. File, sand, and clean up all edges so the ring form is comfortable and shaped the way you want. (I used a half-round file to smooth the edges of the inner ring band by giving them a gentle curve.)

Assembling the Ring Top

1. Select five copper washers of various sizes. Punch each washer with a center punch or an awl to mark a location for drilling. Aligning the holes is not important; stagger the holes if possible so the disks stack irregularly. Drill a hole in each disk, starting with small bits and working up to larger ones, until the hole size fits the sterling silver wire and allows the washers to spin freely on the wire.

2. Clean up the copper washers as needed, and finish their surfaces as desired. (I filed the raw disk edges smooth and gave them a slightly rounded shape. I also used sandpaper and a kitchen scrub pad to give the copper a matte surface.)

3. Use a tube cutter to cut six very small sections of sterling silver tubing. These are tiny spacers, each just a few millimeters in length. (If you want even spacing, make all the sections of tubing the same measurement. I opted for irregular spacing and cut the tubing without precise measurements.) Sand the cut edges to remove burrs.

4. Cut a 1½-inch (3.8 cm) piece of sterling silver wire. Straighten it with a burnisher on a steel block, and file one end totally flat. Using medium solder, solder the wire to the top of the ring band. Pickle, sand, and finish the band as desired, being careful with the wire stem. (I finished my band with 320-, 400-, and 600-grit sandpapers and a kitchen scrub pad.)

5. To straighten and harden the wire stem, burnish and gently hammer the wire while rotating it on a steel block.

6. If desired, patina the ring and tube spacers in a liver of sulfur solution, and then finish the metal with a brass brush.

7. Stack the tubing spacers and disks onto the wire stem, starting and ending with a spacer. Trim the remaining wire end to the depth of the hole in the half-drilled pearl.

8. Carefully holding the stack of disks and spacers taut, hammer and flay out the wire end tip until it lodges tightly in the pearl hole. The pearl can also been secured with glue if desired.

Insight

I'm trained as a designer so I like looking at parts and seeing what can be made from them. It's mind opening to me rather than constricting. I didn't worry about whether or not my sketches were in my style. I just pushed myself to try to have fun and do something different for me. Between a lot of life changes and the decision to relocate my life 2,000 miles away, I'm not feeling the most creatively focused at the moment. In my own sketches, though, I got most excited about the pieces that had movement. They captured some of my innermost feelings (not intentionally) and felt the freshest. My final project didn't use many of the provided materials or much wire (a personal favorite of mine), but it stayed true to my simple, clean design aesthetic while being sculptural and conceptual.

Ultimately, working on this project that isn't in my typical medium of wire got me to do more sketches in a series that I want to develop that is all about balance. It got me out of my comfort zone, and it will be a good breaking out point for me. I'm setting aside more time for non-production studio time to get back in touch with my artistic explorations, which is a very different approach from the business of running a production studio.

artist: Kathy Frey

Created by **Sara Westermark**
Design Number V

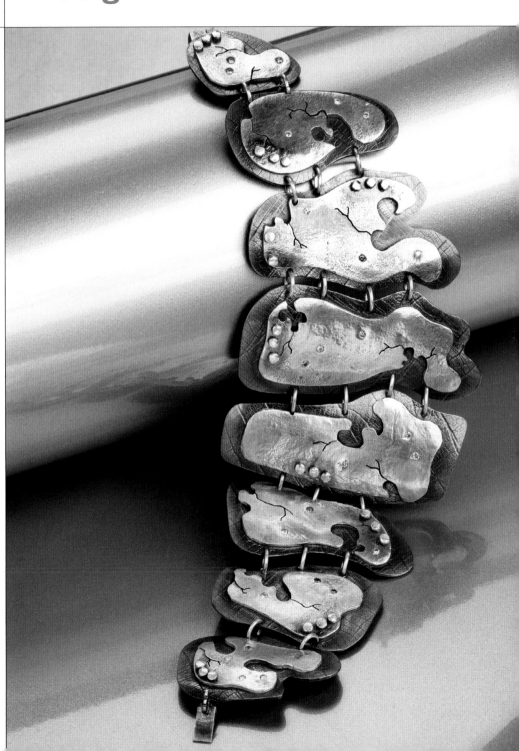

delicate parts create
a bold whole...drama
packed into functional
elements...diamonds pop
amid patinaed layers

Materials & Tools

Photocopied template, page 127
Heavy cardstock
Bench tool kit, page 6
Soldering kit, page 6
Craft paint

Wildcard

24 champagne diamonds,
1.65 mm, VS quality

From the Box

Method

Making the Links

1. Transfer the photocopied template onto a piece of heavy cardstock. Cut out the individual pieces, and label them "sterling" with the numbers 1 through 8. Trace the "sterling" cardstock pieces onto a second piece of cardstock, leaving 2 mm around all edges. Cut out the individual pieces, and label them "copper" with the numbers 1 through 8.

2. Scribe the "sterling" cardstock pieces onto the sterling silver sheet, arranging them in the same configuration as they are depicted in the template. (Set aside all leftover sterling silver scrap. You will need it to make the box clasp.) Repeat process for the "copper" cardstock pieces and the copper sheet.

3. Use a jeweler's saw to cut out the shapes scribed on the sterling and copper sheets. These are the bracelet links. Saw out a series of indented shapes and thin saw lines on each silver link. File and sand all edges.

4. Texture the sterling silver by moving a bushy torch flame over the links in a circular motion. This raises the fine silver to the surface, making it uneven and bumpy. Pickle the textured silver links. Brush them with a brass brush. File and sand their edges.

5. Roll the copper links through the rolling mill, embossing both sides with a leaf texture.

"Before I knew what the exact materials were going to be, I decided that I wanted to make the biggest piece possible out of sterling."

Layering & Embellishing the Links

1. Cut 28 pieces of sterling silver tubing, each 3 mm long. Solder three tubing pieces to the backs of each of the six smaller silver links with medium solder. Solder five pieces of tubing to the backs of both of the large silver links with medium solder. File each piece of tubing to the correct length so it can pass through the copper links, and rivet the two layers together.

2. Paint the ends of the sterling silver tubing with craft paint. Carefully position the corresponding copper links on top of the tubes to transfer the paint. On the copper links, center punch the middle of each paint circle, and drill holes at the punched point. The holes should be just big enough for the tubing to fit through.

3. Feed the silver tubes through the holes in the copper links. Hammer the rivets to fasten the sheet metal layers.

4. Drill a pattern of small holes through each link for the decorative rivets. Drill three additional holes through each link to hold the flush set diamonds. Mark positions for the jump rings on the copper edges of the links. Center punch and drill holes at the marked points.

5. Cut ½-inch (1.3 cm) lengths of the 20-gauge silver wire to use as the decorative rivets. (For this project, the designer used 26 decorative rivets.) Melt one end of each rivet wire into a ball, and hammer it on a riveting block. Rivet the balled and hammered wires through the layered sterling and copper links.

6. Use a rawhide hammer and a bracelet mandrel to slightly curve the links so the bracelet will fit the wrist.

Creating the Box Clasp

1. Roll the leftover sterling silver sheet through a rolling mill until the scraps measure 24 or 26 gauge. Cut a 1.3 x 1 cm rectangle for the top of the box. Build a true, 2 mm tall rectangle from the thinned sterling sheet. Solder the rectangle onto the top of the box with hard solder. Make all the edges precise 90° angles. Trim the edges flush with a saw, then file and sand them smooth. Saw an opening in one narrow end of the rectangle, and notch the top of the opening.

2. Cut a strip of silver to use as the tongue for the box clasp. The width of the strip should fit inside the opening of the box. The strip's length should be twice as long as the interior of the box. Solder a latch onto the strip. Fit the tongue into the open box. (This should be a tight fit.) File away excess metal.

3. Cut a 1.3 x 1 cm piece of the thinned silver sheet to use as the bottom of the box clasp. Solder this sheet to the rectangle with medium solder. Trim the edges flush, and pickle the box.

4. With easy solder, solder the box clasp onto the far left link of the bracelet with the notched side facing up. Solder the tongue for the box clasp onto the far right link with the latch facing up.

Finishing the Bracelet

1. Make approximately 21 jump rings out of sterling silver wire. Connect the links of the bracelet with the jump rings. Solder the rings closed with easy solder. Wiggle the rings to check for strength and flexibility.

2. Pickle the bracelet for the last time. Tumble the bracelet with steel shot and a polishing solution.

3. To flush set the diamonds, first redrill the premade holes with a flame tip burr that is slightly smaller than the diameter of the diamond. Then, make the seats for the stones with a hart or a stone-setting burr. Place one diamond in each seat, "snapping" it into the setting.

4. Push the metal onto the diamonds with a graver or the tip of a burnisher. Work in a "compass formation" (north, south, east, and west), beginning on one side of each diamond and then pushing down the opposite side. Smooth the metal around each diamond with the burnisher.

5. Oxidize the bracelet, and brush it with steel wool.

Insight

I love the challenge of working within set limits—I feel that it charges my creative thoughts. Before I knew what the exact materials were going to be, I decided that I wanted to make the biggest piece possible out of sterling. I had a basic idea, but I had to adapt it to fit the 3-inch (7.6 cm) square of the sterling that was included in the box of raw materials. I began to make sketches of how I was going to maximize the surface area of the sterling. Probably the hardest part for me was not limited materials, but reproducing my sketch without making last-minute changes.

artist: Sara Westermark

Created by **Davide Bigazzi**

Design Number VI

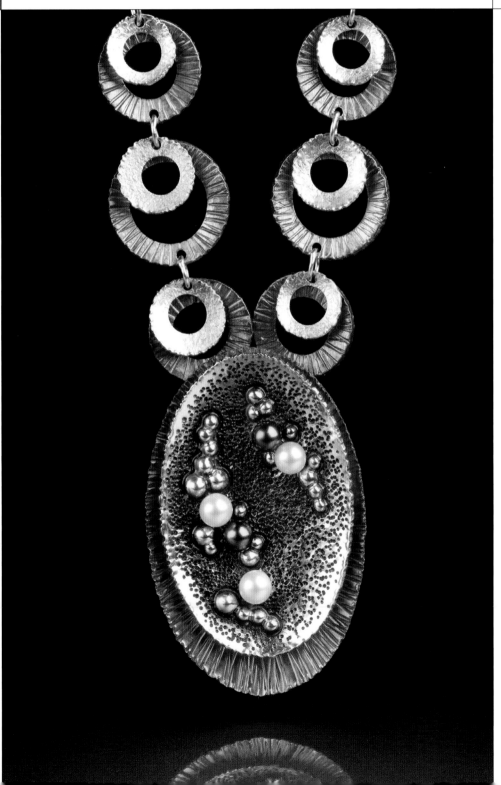

elevates raw materials with technique...a very modern application of repoussé...achieves more from the materials than the individual supplies

Tools & Materials
Bench tool kit, page 6
Soldering kit, page 6
Stencil with oval shapes
Disk cutter
Rough steel for texture surface
Pitch bowl
Liver of sulfur

Wildcard
None

From the Box

Method
1. Using a rolling mill, thin the sterling silver sheet and the copper sheet to 22 gauge.

2. Select an oval stencil that is approximately 3.3 x 4.5 cm, and trace its shape onto the sterling silver sheet. Use a jeweler's saw to cut out the silver oval. Select an oval stencil that is approximately 3.7 x 5.6 cm, and trace its shape onto the copper sheet. Use a jeweler's saw to cut out the copper oval.

3. Use a rolling mill to thin the remaining sterling silver sheet to 24 gauge.

Creating the Chain
1. Using a disk cutter, cut out 19 disks from the silver sheet, each 1.3 cm in diameter. Using a 9.5 mm punch, cut out the center of 14 of the silver disks. Texture the disks with a peen hammer, and saw one side open. Cut out the center of the remaining five disks with a 6.3 mm punch. Hammer the disks against a piece of rough steel to texture. Drill a hole in each of these five disks.

2. Cut out seven 1.1 cm disks from the silver sheet with the disk cutter. Use a 6.3 mm punch to cut out the center of these disks. Hammer them against a piece of rough steel to texture. Drill a hole in each of these seven disks.

3. Cut out 16 disks from the copper sheet, each 1.3 cm in diameter. Use a 9.5 mm punch to cut out the center of these disks. Texture them with a peen hammer.

4. Texture the surface of the 14 commercial copper washers with a peen hammer. Texture the outer edge of the washers with a triangular file. Drill two holes in each washer, directly across from each other. (These washers will later be connected with jump rings.)

5. Make 16 jump rings with the sterling silver wire, each 3.7 mm in diameter. Use the jump rings to link two strands of six commercial copper washers, adding one handmade and drilled silver "washer" to embellish each connection.

6. Make two strands of 14 handmade "washers," alternating a precut silver one with a copper one. Solder the silver washers closed.

7. Use a jump ring to connect a commercial copper washer to the silver end of each handmade "washer" strand. Cut and slightly open one commercial copper washer at the end of the strand to use as the clasp. Use jump rings to connect the other end of each handmade "washer" strand to a strand of commercial washers.

Creating & Attaching the Pendant

1. Using a sand bag and a raising hammer, hammer the sterling silver oval slightly concave. Do the same to the copper oval.

2. Place the silver oval in the pitch bowl with the convex side facing up. With two sizes of small rounded punches, repoussé a pattern of half spheres on the surface of the metal. Remove the silver oval from the pitch. Burn off the pitch, and anneal the metal.

3. Place the silver oval in the pitch with the concave side facing up. Using a pointed punch or a nail, texture the surface of the metal around the raised spheres. Remove the silver oval from the pitch. With a triangular file, texture the outer edge of the silver oval.

4. Cut five 3 mm pieces of sterling silver wire to use for the pearl settings. Solder the wires vertically onto the silver oval.

5. Hammer the surface of the copper oval with a peen hammer to create texture. With a triangular file, texture the outer edge of the copper oval.

6. Solder the silver oval on top of the copper oval. Cut one jump ring in half. On each end of the washer chain, feed one half jump ring through the drilled hole in the last link. Solder the half jump rings to the back of the copper oval. The pendant is now attached to the chain.

7. Brush the entire necklace with a brass brush. Apply liver of sulfur solution to the silver oval, and polish. Glue the pearls to the prepared settings.

Insight

I looked forward to the challenge. I found the constraints motivating. The process of creating is always inspiring, and I enjoyed participating.

artist: Davide Bigazzi

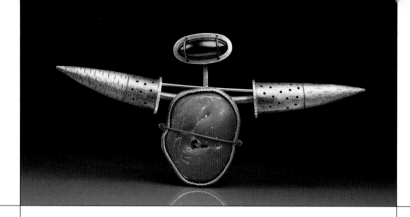

Design Number VII

Created by **Thomas Mann**

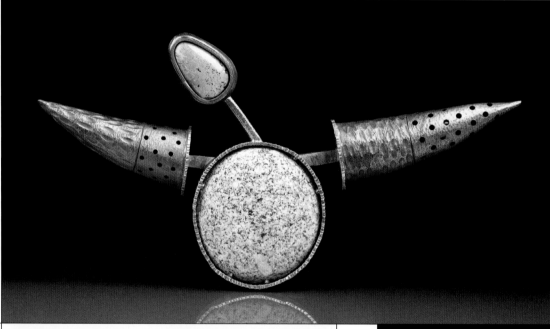

"Okay, so what I'm gonna do is make as many pieces out of the allotted materials as I can."

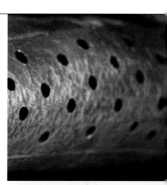

pushes materials as far as they can go…hollow pods define space… finishes provide a worn warmth

Tools & Materials

Bench tool kit, page 6
Soldering kit, page 6
Photocopied template, page 126
Glue
Negative half-round shaping blocks
Goldsmithing hammer
Rotary file cylinder
Carbide burrs, ball and cone
Snap-on sanding disks
Liver of sulfur

Wildcard

River stones

Method

1. Cut thin strips of the sterling silver sheet. Laminate the strips together with solder to form a thick square wire. Forge the laminated silver into 6-gauge square wire. Cut strips of the silver and copper sheet to use as bezel wire for your stones. Solder the strips end to end, creating long, flat bezel wires.

2. Use a rolling mill to thin the copper sheet to 20 or 22 gauge. Glue the photocopied pod template to the copper sheet, and saw out the selected form or forms.

3. With a cross peen hammer, forge a line down the center of a pod. This forces the metal to begin curving upward.

4. Move the evolving pod form to the half-round shaping blocks for further definition and to bring the edges of the pod closer.

5. With light taps from the flat face of a ball peen rivet hammer, gently and delicately close the edges of the pod. Solder the seam of the pod, and pickle the form.

6. Place the closed pod in the half-round block. With the flat face of the rivet hammer, gently tap the pod to coax it from its oval shape into a round, tube shape.

7. Repeat steps 3 through 6 to create as many pod forms as desired for your design. Saw each pod into halves or thirds.

From the Box

8. Measure the diameter of the open end of the pods. Saw or cut sterling silver disks to this measurement, one for each portion of pod. Solder the cut end of the pods onto the silver disks. Solder a length of square wire to the center of each silver disk.

9. Design and fabricate a bezel for the stone. (Note: The bezels in the featured projects aren't closed in the traditional manner. They all employ either tabs or wire strapping to keep the stones in position.)

10. Finish the surface of all pods; here, a cylinder rotary file carbide burr was used. Carve details into the pods and the bezel with the edge of a knife and/or ball and cone carbide burrs.

11. Design and fabricate other design elements as desired. In this project, twisted wires were soldered around the perimeter of the bezel and looped at the end. A thinner wire was fed through one loop, strung with a pearl, and then fed through the next loop. This process was repeated for the whole circle. The ends of the wire were wrapped to secure. The variations for this project feature other design choices, such as the addition of a second unconventionally set stone.

12. Solder the bezels, other design elements (as desired), and the handmade pin findings in place. Clean up all solder joints with a snap-on sanding disk on the flexible shaft.

13. Finish the metal surfaces with steel wool. Immerse the brooch in a warm liver of sulfur solution to blacken the metal. Dry the brooch, and rub the surface again with steel wool to highlight sections.

14. Mount the stones and secure their settings. Cut the pin stems and fit them into their findings.

Note: As stated in his "insight," Thomas Mann endeavored to create as many pieces as possible from the provided materials. His ring and pendant pieces are pictured, but instructions are not included.

Insight

As I viewed the materials in the box, I thought, "man, this is like *Chopped* on the Food Network." Okay, so what I'm gonna do is make as many pieces out of the allotted materials as I can. How many pins can I get out of this material resource?

First I experimented using my own materials, making several synclastic pod forms to get the technique refreshed in my head and hands. I figured out how many forms I'd need and their sizes. I knew I could use a wildcard and that was always going to be beach rocks. I've been using them in various forms for years, and I still love them.

After approximately 30 hours of work, I ended up with 11 pieces and just a little bit of leftover scrap. My only regret is that I didn't use the silver mesh!

I see this body of work as having what I would call a "Techno-Natura" look and feel. Natural forms and materials are referenced and juxtaposed with apparently man-made elements that reference the structural steel components of bridges and buildings.

artist: Thomas Mann

Design Number VIII

Created by **Rebecca Hannon**

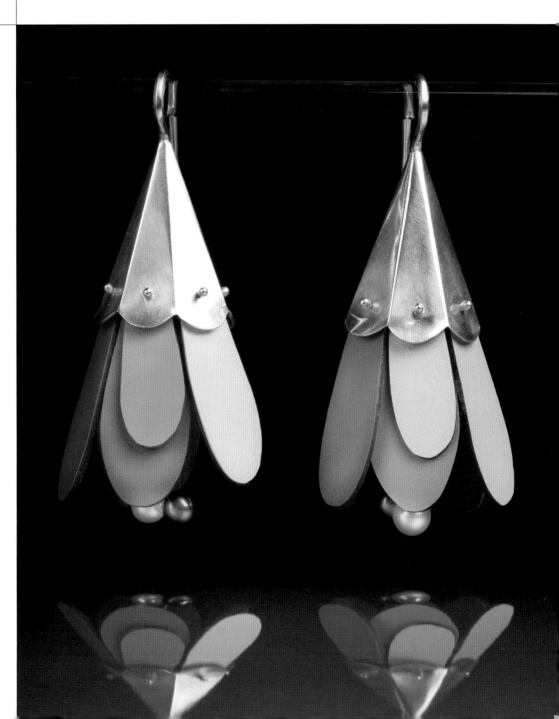

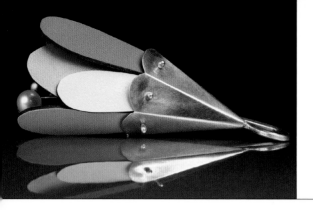

Design Number VIII

bold, unmatched, and
vibrant...wildcard offers
color and character...
lyrical shape lifts up

Materials & Tools
Bench tool kit, page 6
Soldering kit, page 6
Photocopied template,
   page 127 (make 2 copies)

Wildcard
Countertop laminate sample chips*

*Colorful and strong countertop
laminate sample chips can be found
at home supply centers or recycled
from an architect's office.*

From the Box

Method

1. Use a jeweler's saw to cut out a 3 x 1½-inch (7.6 x 3.8 cm) rectangle of sterling silver sheet. Roll the rectangle lengthwise through the rolling mill, thinning it to 24 gauge. Anneal the silver rectangle.

2. Affix the photocopied templates to the sterling silver rectangle with a glue stick.

3. Cut out both sterling silver forms with a jeweler's saw. Remove the point of each scribed cone as show in the template. (This makes folding the form easier and smoother and creates the small opening in each form that is later needed.)

4. Run a triangular needle file down the five scribed quadrant lines on each silver form, creating deep score lines for folding. File the edges of both forms.

5. Fold the silver forms into cones. Solder each seam, and then pickle the forms. Shape them with your fingers, and sand the soldered seams. If the hole on the top of the cone has filled with solder, drill it open.

6. Cut two 3-inch (7.6 cm) pieces of sterling silver wire. Create a closed jump ring on one end of each wire. Feed a wire up through the inside of each cone.

7. Holding the wire taught, cleanly solder it on the top of the cone. Repeat for the second cone and wire. Pickle and rinse the cones. Harden the ear wires by burnishing them on a steel plate.

8. Using a 1 mm bit, drill a centered hole near the arched base of each quadrant on the cone. The rivet holes will hold on the petals.

9. Cut 12 pieces of sterling silver wire, each 1 inch (2.5 cm) long. Use a torch to melt a ball on one end of each piece of wire.

10. Draw a 6-inch (15.2 cm) piece of sterling silver wire down to 25 gauge. Anneal the thinned wire. (This wire will become the pearl "stamen.") Cut the wire in half, and feed one length through the inner jump ring on both cone forms. Gently twist the wire so it hangs in the center of the cone.

11. Draw petal shapes on various colors of countertop laminate sample chips. Make sure that the top of each petal fits inside the quadrants of the silver cone. (In this project, nine petals were needed for each earring. The quadrants on the cone alternate between holding a single petal and a double petal.)

12. Position a petal or a layer of two petals inside the cone where you would like it to hang. Wedge the assembly onto your bench pin, and drill a hole through the existing hole in the cone. This method creates perfectly placed holes in the petals. Repeat this process to drill all laminate petals.

13. Insert a balled wire rivet through the front of a cone quadrant and its petal or petals. Bend a small circle of wire inside the cone to secure the rivet. Repeat this process on all quadrants of both earrings.

14. To form the pearl stamen, wrap two pearls on each of the wires that are hanging inside the cones. Snip off any excess wire. Bend the ear wires into shape, and snip off any excess.

Insight

To be honest, I was actually surprised that there weren't a few crazier materials included in the box—like a 5-pound beach stone or a tin can or a piece of Astro turf. The materials were straightforward jewelry supplies, so I was happy to be able to throw in one of my own wacky materials as the wildcard. I chose Formica chips, always available in fantastic, long wearing colors and, in this case, recycled from an architect's office.

artist: Rebecca Hannon

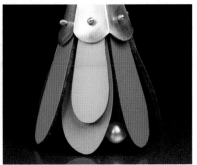

Created by **Danielle Miller-Gilliam**

Design Number IX

forging organic forms...

finishes in high contrast...

kinetic pearls...expertly

integrated clasp

Materials & Tools

Bench tool kit, page 6
Soldering kit, page 6
Photocopied design templates,
  page 127
Swage forming block, stake, mandrel
  and/or items for forming arcs
Tube-cutting jig
Diamond burr, bullet or cone shaped
Liver of sulfur solution
Rubber cement and paper
Silicon carbide separating disks or
  aluminum oxide cut-off wheels
Cross peen hammer
Dowels for making jump rings
Radial bristle disks, 80-grit
Cotton-tipped swab
Pearl adhesive

Wildcard

7 freshwater pearls, fully drilled

Method

Constructing the Open Pod Forms

1. Cut the copper sheet into four 9.5 x 0.7 cm strips and twelve 3.8 x 0.7 cm strips.

2. To create thicker strips, sweat-solder matching pairs together down their long edges. After soldering all the pieces, you will have made two double-wide strips that are 9.5 cm long and six double-wide strips that are 3.8 cm long. Pickle and rinse the strips. File all edges clean and straight.

3. Form all copper strips into arcs. Use a swage forming block, a plastic mandrel, and a rawhide mallet to bend each of the short strips. To bend the long strips, you may need to improvise. None of my mandrels or stakes had the correct curve, so I used a sturdy container with the appropriate circumference. If using a container, make sure it is strong enough to withstand mallet blows.

4. Fit two arcs of the same length together to form a pod shape, and solder their ends. After soldering all arcs in this manner, you will have one large and six small pod shapes. Pickle the metal.

5. File the top and bottom edges of the pod forms, sloping down to the points of each and rounding all the edges. Once you achieve the

From the Box

desired shape, sand each piece to a 400-grit finish. This sculpting gives the shape a less bulky, more sensual form.

Expert Tip: If you have a polishing machine, use a quick finish cutting compound. It functions like sandpaper and comes in 120, 220, and 400 grit. Apply it to a tight-weave muslin wheel, just as you would polishing compound. (Don't forget to use a dust mask and safety glasses!)

---

6. Using a tubing jig, cut 13 pieces of sterling silver tubing that are each 3 mm long. Determine the backs of the pod forms. Solder the small tubes onto the backs of the pod forms as close to their points as possible. For the small pods, solder a tube on each point. For the large pod, solder a single tube at one point. Pickle the pods. With a barrette needle file, shape the small pieces of tubing to mimic the angle of the pod.

7. Mark and drill a hole through one side of each of the small pods. (I like to do this in a different location on each pod to add visual interest.) Determine the location of the wires on the large pod, and mark and drill eight holes.

8. Cut six pieces of copper wire that are each 5 mm long. Fit the wires into the drilled holes in the small pods. Most of the wire should protrude into the pod's negative space, and just a small bit should be left on the outside. Solder the wire into the hole, applying the solder to the outside bit of wire. Pickle the forms. File and then sand the excess wire flush to the outside of the pod shape. Using a diamond burr in a flexible shaft, put an even texture on the inside of all the pod shapes. (This detail creates a subtle contrast between the smooth outside and textured inside.)

9. Thoroughly clean the pods with soapy water to remove all dirt and oils. Wearing rubber gloves and working in a well-ventilated area, dissolve a pea-sized piece of liver of sulfur in warm water. Soak the pod forms in the liquid mixture for a minute or so. Rinse with warm water, and brush the metal with a brass brush. Repeat this procedure several times, building up a rich, dark surface.

Creating the Scored and Bent Leaf Forms

1. Adhere photocopied leaf templates to the sterling sheet with rubber cement. Carefully saw out the shapes and file the edges smooth.

2. There are several ways to score and bend. For this project, I used a grinding method. Secure one of the leaf shapes onto a scrap wood block with masking tape. Scribe a straight centerline from point to point. Using a metal straightedge as a starting guide, score along the centerline with a cutting/separating disk attachment in a flexible shaft. Do not press hard—let the disk do the work for you. Carefully go back and forth along the score line, then turn the wood block to reverse your starting direction. This ensures that your cut will be an even depth. Continue to score until the groove is approximately three quarters of the way through the thickness of the metal. (You should start to see a slight raised line on the other side of the sheet.) Since the groove is U shaped, you'll now need to use a square needle file to remove some of the walls to make a V-shaped groove. Bend the metal at the score line. Flow solder into the groove to reinforce it. Pickle the metal. Repeat this step for all leaf shapes.

3. One at a time, place the bent silver leaves on the edge of a steel bench block. With a rounded cross peen hammer, gently hammer the outside edge of the silver in a radial pattern. The hammering will cause the silver shape to arc up toward the points from the center bend.

4. To make the hook for the clasp, cut a slightly tapered strip from the leftover sterling silver sheet that is 3.2 cm long and approxi-

mately 3 mm wide at its widest point. File the edges clean, round off the narrow end, and file the widest end to a V shape. Using pliers, shape the tapered strip into a graceful hook. Sand and clean the metal.

5. Make a coil with the sterling silver wire, and cut 20 jump rings, each 5 mm in diameter. Solder two jump rings into the groove under each leaf, one ring close to each point. Solder the V-shaped end of the hook into the groove of one of the smaller leaf forms. Pickle the silver leaves.

6. Put a consistent finish on the fronts and backs of the silver leaves. I used a stack of three radial bristle disks on a flexible shaft screw mandrel to create a matte finish.

Assembling the Necklace

1. Link the copper pods and the silver leaves together with the remaining jump rings. Quickly and carefully solder the jump rings closed. Using a cotton swab, carefully apply pickle to the solder joints, and rinse with water. (Too much heat and pickle will affect the patina on the copper pods.)

2. Straighten a length of sterling silver wire and cut four pieces, each approximately 1¼ inches (3.2 cm) long. Ball up one end of each wire with a torch. Pickle and rinse the balled wires. Fit the wires though the holes of the large copper pod and thread the pearls onto the wires. (You may need to enlarge the holes in the pearls to fit on the 20-gauge wire. If so, try using a #65 [0.89 mm] bit.) Quickly, ball up the other end of the wire. Using a cotton-tipped swab, carefully apply pickle to the discolored balls, and rinse with water. (You must act quickly when balling up these last wires. Too much heat will burn the pearl, and the pickle will remove the nacre.) Be sure that the posts inside the small pod forms are clean and dry. Glue single-hole pearls onto the posts.

Insight

When I first received the box of supplies, I was very excited and somewhat stumped. I wanted to create something that was reminiscent of my signature style, but the supplies in the box were not my usual materials. Many of my designs begin with square or rectangular wire, and I never use copper sheet, mesh, or washers. I let it all simmer for a while, and when I decided I would sweat-solder pieces of copper sheet together to create my own rectangular strips, the ideas began to flow. I wanted to explore the use of solid and negative space, as my work normally does, but I also wanted to play with scale by making a slightly larger piece than I normally do. I changed my mind several times before I settled on my final design. More pearls were an obvious choice for my wildcard item, and they fit in perfectly with my black and white color scheme.

artist: Danielle Miller-Gilliam

Created by **Robert Dancik**

Design Number X

faux bone tells a tale...

fold-formed texture...

a kind of futuristic relic

Tools & Materials

Bench tool kit, page 6
Soldering kit, page 6
Photocopied template, page 127
Saw blades for faux bone
Stamps, bolts, texture tools
Electric engraver, scribe, craft knife
   or similar for scratching faux bone
Acrylic paint and/or shoe polish
Vise (optional)
Polishing wheel with plain muslin
   buff (optional)

Wildcard

Faux bone, 8 inches (20.3 cm)
square, 6 mm thick

From the Box

Method
Preparing the Major Elements

1. Mark a 14.6 cm circle on the faux bone sheet. Mark a 6.9 cm concentric circle inside the first circle. Cut out the outer and the inner circles. File and round all edges.

2. Cut out a 2 x 6-inch (5 x 15.2 cm) piece of copper sheet. Anneal the sheet, and roll it through the rolling mill until it measures approximately 18 inches (45.7 cm) long. (The thinned sheet should be about 24 gauge.) With each pass through the rolling mill, be sure to turn over the sheet and start rolling at the other end. Also, anneal the sheet after every other pass.

3. Cut out a ¾ x 6-inch (1.9 x 15.2 cm) piece of copper sheet. Roll the copper to a thickness of 26 gauge (or a bit thinner), annealing and turning the sheet as described in step 2. The rolled strip will be approximately 18 to 20 inches (45.7 to 50.8 cm) long.

4. Cut out a ½ x 3-inch (1.3 x 7.6 cm) piece of sterling silver sheet. Roll the silver through the mill, annealing and turning the sheet, until it is approximately 10 inches (25.4 cm) long.

5. Cut the 2-inch-wide (5 cm) copper strip into two 6½-inch (16.5 cm) lengths and two 2½-inch (6.4 cm) lengths. Texture the copper pieces using textured hammers, hammers of various shapes and sizes, stamps, the threaded sides of bolts, and any other mark-making methods you like. You can also turn the pieces over and hammer them against various materials such as concrete, rough metal castings, blocks of rusted metal, rocks, etc. The object here is to give the metal the sort of variations one might find in a landscape. Anneal the metal as you texture it so it won't crack (unless, of course, you want cracks in your piece).

Creating the Fold-Formed Copper Strips

1. Position the copper strips to cover the faux bone blank, with the longer pieces overlapping the shorter ones. Label the back of each copper piece so you can reassemble them after fold forming.

2. Fold form one of the 15.2 cm lengths of copper, trying to make a fold across the width of the piece, about 3.8 cm in from each end. (This fold will intersect a short copper strip.) Form other folds along the length of the copper, letting the lines overlap as desired. Anneal the strip as needed, but don't pickle it.

3. Select one of the shorter lengths of copper that is adjacent to the fold-formed length. Extend the fold lines from the long copper piece onto the shorter one, and form additional folds as desired. Place the other long piece next to this shorter piece, and extend the fold lines. Repeat this process, making sure the fold-formed lines run continuously from the short to the long copper pieces.

Preparing & Refining the Additional Components

1. Cut 20 to 25 pieces of copper wire, each ¾ inch (1.9 cm) long. Melt a ball on one end of each wire. These will be your rivets.

2. Position one short copper piece on the faux bone blank. Using a 0.81 mm bit, drill one hole and insert one wire to hold the copper in place, but don't rivet it yet. Drill a second hole, and insert another wire. Overlap one of the long pieces of copper, align the folds, drill holes, and insert rivet wires as above. Continue with the remaining pieces of copper, making sure the folds line up.

3. Turn over the bracelet and trace the outline of the faux bone blank onto the back of the copper pieces. Remove the metal, saw along the traced lines, and file and sand the pieces. (With all the annealing for the fold forming, the copper should have an excellent heat patina by now. This coloration will come to a wonderful luster if rubbed with a brass brush.)

4. Measure the inside diameter of the bracelet, and cut the silver strip to fit. Solder the ends of the silver strip together with hard solder. File and sand the silver to a soft finish. (This is the sleeve that covers the inside edge of the bracelet.)

Making the Hammered Silver Circle

1. Cut two strips of sterling silver sheet, each ½ inch (1.3 cm) wide. Roll the strips to a thickness of 22 gauge. (Each thinned strip should be approximately 6 inches (15.2 cm) long.) Cut each strip into two 3-inch (7.6 cm) pieces.

2. Working on the edge of a bench block or anvil, hammer one edge of each strip with a cross peen hammer to curve it into a quarter circle. Place the strips on the faux bone blank to check for the right curvature—the inside edges should match. (Work slowly, and keep checking the strips so you don't forge them past the curve.) Divide the bracelet blank into quarters. Mark the silver strips so each one measures one-quarter of the diameter of the bracelet's interior hole. Cut the strips to length.

3. With the forged side of one silver strip facing up, use the template to create an arch.

"I called upon my background as a land surveyor and drawing maps and decided to make a bracelet that was both a model of a landscape and a map of the territory."

Mark the other three silver strips in this fashion. Cut, file, and sand the strips.

4. Solder the narrow end of one silver strip to the wide end of the second strip to form a half circle. Continue with the other strips to form a circle that is the same size as the interior cutout of the bracelet. File and sand the silver circle, and finish the outside edges with a checkering file, if desired. (I also used an electric engraver to texture the silver.)

Preparing the Pearl Cages

1. Determine where you want the three caged pearls to sit on the bracelet. (One location must be directly above one of the long copper pieces on the other side of the bracelet so its hole can go all the way through the piece.) Trace the interior hole of a copper washer onto the faux bone at each location. (Three different size washers were used on this bracelet.) Cut out the holes, and file and sand the edges.

2. Cut three pieces of the fine silver mesh, each just a bit smaller than the copper washers. Slightly dome four washers in a dapping block, and then dome the mesh inside the washer domes. Sand, texture, and patina the domed copper washers and mesh as desired.

Assembling & Finishing the Bracelet

1. Finish the side of the bracelet that will not be covered with copper sheet by sanding the faux bone with 400- then 600-grit wet sandpaper and lots of water. After sanding with the 600-grit paper, turn the sheet over and vigorously rub the faux bone with the paper to softly polish its surface. Rub the faux bone on your hand and then on a pant leg to bring up a shine. Alternately, you can buff the surface on a plain, loose muslin buff with no polishing compound.

2. Rivet one of the small, fold-formed copper pieces to the bracelet, adding rivets where needed. (You need to attach the copper pieces in order so the large pieces overlap the small ones.)

3. When you reach the hole for the pearl that goes all the way through the bracelet, mark the copper and cut the hole. Rivet one of the domed washer cages (mesh inside) over the hole on the outside of the copper. Place a pearl in the cage. Rivet a domed washer cage on the faux bone side of the same hole. Continue riveting the fold-formed copper strips to the bracelet. (Note: Before hammering the copper rivets on the faux bone side, bevel the holes with a triangular scraper or a slightly larger drill bit so the rivet heads will be flush with the faux bone.)

4. Place the silver sleeve inside the bracelet's interior hole. Slide the forged silver circle over the sleeve, and adjust it to lie flat against

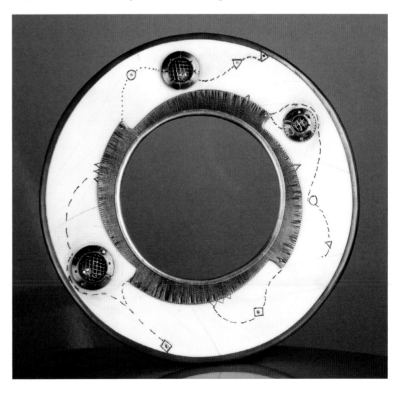

the faux bone. Using 0.87 mm bit, drill a hole in one corner of the forged silver circle, and insert a rivet to hold it in place. Repeat this process on the other three corners. Complete the rivets on both sides of the bracelet.

5. Holding the bracelet parallel to and 6 mm from the bench, tap the edge of the silver sleeve to start pushing it over the copper side of the bracelet. Tap at opposite sides, and work your way around until the silver sleeve is leaning outward. Turn the bracelet over, and repeat this process. Keep turning the bracelet and hammering the sleeve until it lies flat against the silver ring on one side of the bracelet and the textured copper on the other.

6. Measure the thickness of the outer edge of the bracelet. Using the copper sheet thinned in step 3 on page 41, cut a strip that is approximately 6 mm wider than this measurement. File and sand the strip. Wrap the strip around the perimeter of the bracelet. Measure, cut, and solder the strip, forming a ring that fits tight against the bracelet. Patina the copper ring as desired. Position the copper ring so it protrudes about 3 mm past each side of the bracelet. Using your fingers, gently fold the copper ring over the edge of the bracelet. (The copper is thin enough to be pressed down most of the way with finger pressure.) Hammer the bent copper ring with a dead-blow hammer or rawhide mallet.

7. Place a pearl or two in the two remaining holes on the faux bone side of the bracelet. Rivet a domed washer cage over each hole.

8. Using an electric etcher, scribe, craft knife, or similar tool, scratch the surface of the faux bone as desired. If needed, re-sand the surface to remove any burrs that arise in the process, and repolish the faux bone. To color the incised lines, rub in and immediately rub off paint, shoe polish, or other pigment. Give the bracelet a final buffing on your pant leg or on an electric buff.

Insight

I must admit that when first presented with the invitation to participate in the jewelry design challenge, I was intrigued and excited. I imagined what we might be given—a scrap of wood, a bit of silver (it is, after all, rather expensive), some chewing gum, a tin can, maybe a length of wire or shoe laces, perhaps a map, and some broken glass? When I realized that the box would contain traditional materials, I immediately thought of several possible forms to pursue, and my mind raced around for quite a while, moving in various directions. When it was time to put pencil to paper, I let myself draw and draw and then draw some more. I called upon my background as a land surveyor and drawing maps and decided to make a bracelet that was both a model of a landscape and a map of the territory. I could roll the copper thin enough to fold-form for the landscape and then draw on the Faux Bone—my wildcard of choice—for the map. After a lot of sketches, I had a fairly accurate working drawing. When the materials arrived, I found that their physical characteristics actually helped my process and suggested certain modifications that I built into the finished piece, knowing that I needed to follow my drawing (at least in good part). All in all, I quite liked the whole idea of having an "assignment" with certain parameters defined. It forced me to look at materials I am familiar with in another light and to try a different procedural approach to a form of adornment I've made many times before.

artist: Robert Dancik

Design Number XI

Created by **Bob Ebendorf**

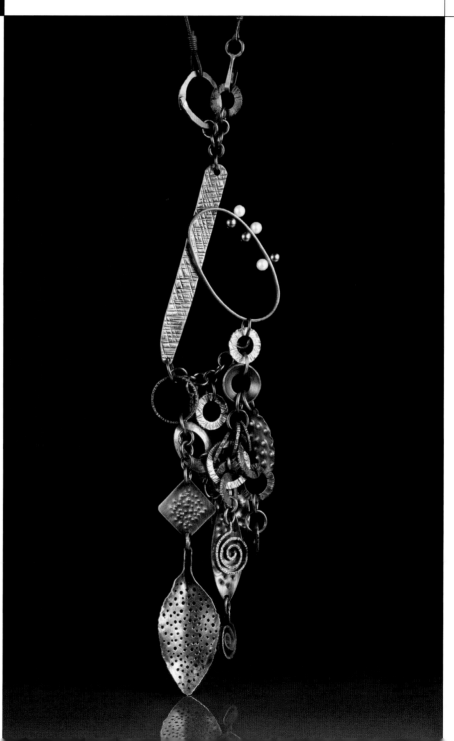

Design Number XI

multitude of textures...

a sense of play...

asymmetrical elements

Materials & Tools
Bench tool kit, page 6
Soldering kit, page 6
Texturing and forming tools
Liver of sulfur
Pearl epoxy

Wildcard
None

From the Box

Method

1. Design an assortment of interesting shapes you wish to explore. There are eight sheet forms in this assemblage: a large leaf, a pod, two solid ovals, two pierced ovals, a diamond, and a long rectangle with one rounded end and one tapered end. Draw your forms on the copper sheet, and cut them out with a jeweler's saw.

2. Using a center punch and hammer, establish points on the copper forms where you would like to drill the metal. Each form will need at least one functional hole to accommodate a jump ring, but you may wish to drill decorative holes as well. (Here, the large leaf has a profusion of drilled holes.) Drill the copper forms. If desired, pierce and saw out the interior forms of your copper shapes. (In this project, two ovals have pierced interior ovals.)

3. Use texturing tools, such as hammers, punches, chasing tools, and stamps, to pattern the copper forms as desired. Vary the force of the blow to alter the appearance of the patterns. Forcefully texture each copper washer as well. Give the textured copper pieces more fluid shapes by dapping, punching, or bending them.

4. Cut the leftover copper sheet into narrow strips. Bend one long copper strip into a very large oval. Solder the oval closed. Hammer one end of a short strip to widen it. Bend this strip into a hook for the clasp. Bend one strip into an overlapping circle, and flatten it with a hammer. Bend the remaining strips into various linear forms, such as spirals. Drill a centered hole through the overlapping ends of the ring section of the clasp and near the ends of each linear element.

5. Wrap the copper wire around a 5 to 7 mm mandrel to make a large coil. Saw the coil apart to create jump rings. Solder one jump ring to the clasp hook.

6. Color all the copper elements (the cut forms, the washers, the clasp elements, etc.) as well as some extra length of copper wire in a liver of sulfur solution. Rinse, dry, and buff or brush as desired to remove some of the patina from the top surfaces of the texture.

7. Cut a rivet from the sterling silver wire, and rivet the flattened ring closed.

8. Drill three holes in the large oval copper ring where you want to attach the pearls. Solder the large oval ring on top of the large tapered rectangle. Carefully drill each pearl to fully extend its hole. Cut three lengths of sterling silver wire that are long enough to pass through the large copper oval and serve as a post for a pearl on each side of it. One at a time, place a drop of epoxy on a pearl and mount it on a post. Set this element aside.

9. Consider how you want to assemble the remaining copper elements, bringing them together to formally complete the design. Elements can be linked with single jump rings or multiple jump rings, or washers can be sawed apart and used to link components. Once you have determined a design, connect the copper elements. Use the same reasoning and method to connect the large component with pearls and, at the very top, the clasp.

10. Cut a length of the leather cord to go around the neck. Feed one end of the cord through the jump ring that is attached to the hook clasp, fold the end of the cord back, and tightly wrap the extra oxidized wire around the overlapped cord. Feed the other end of the leather cord through the flattened ring part of the clasp, fold the end of the cord back, and tightly wrap the extra oxidized wire around the overlapped cord.

Insight

My first impression upon receiving the box was that I wanted to use only the supplied elements. I found the challenge of working with just a few materials to be quite exciting. I oftentimes have a tendency to overload, so it was fun to receive an assignment where you work within parameters. This project came at a perfect time to allow me to respond creatively to the challenge, be playful, and enjoy the adventure.

artist: Bob Ebendorf

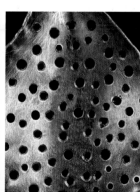

Design Number XII
Created by **Mary Hettmansperger**

> **"Once I picked out my wildcard—
> 26-gauge copper wire—I started
> to feel more comfortable, and my
> creative juices started to flow."**

endless layers and detail...
trapped elements hang
weightless...uses wire like
thread to build connections

Tools & Materials

Bench tool kit, page 6
Torch
Disk cutter
Old pliers
Sharp awl
Bench grinder with
   deburring wheel
Lead-free enamels (optional)

Wildcard

Copper wire, 26 gauge

From the Box

Method

1. Anneal the copper and silver sheets. Use a rolling mill to thin both sheets to approximately 24 gauge. Re-anneal the thinned metal sheets. Roll the copper washers through the mill to thin them. The shapes of the washers will change when thinned, creating a variety of circles and ovals.

2. Use disk cutters or shears to cut circles out of the silver and copper sheets, varying the sizes as desired. Pierce and saw out interior shapes on some of the silver circles to echo the contour of the rolled washers.

3. Texture the metal circles with a hammer, and forge their edges to create an organic, deckled effect. Use a bench grinder with a deburring wheel to smooth the edges of the circles. Gently hammer some of the circles in a dapping block, varying the arcs of the domes.

4. One at a time, heat some of the copper circles with a torch to create a red heat patina. Quench the circles in ice water or in boiling hot water to vary the coloration.

Expert Tip: Painting flux on the backs of the circles as you heat them reduces firescale and allows the red coloration to appear on both sides of the circles.

---

5. Place all of the metal circles, ovals, and washers on your workspace, and begin to formulate a necklace design. Move the elements around and layer them until you are pleased with the arrangement. Determine where and how to connect the elements. (This project uses jump rings, ball rivets, stitches, ties, and tube rivets to join elements.) Drill holes at the points where the connections will be made.

6. Precut an ample supply of jump rings, wire rivets, and tube rivets. Embellish each necklace component as desired through the addition of functional and nonfunctional elements and decoration. Here are some options for customizing each component:

• Add a layer of torch-fired enamel to some of the larger copper pieces.

• Pierce a line of decorative holes across a dome with a sharp awl, and use the outermost holes as functional locations for balled-wire rivets.

• Use multiple jump rings to make a single connection. This increases visual interest and security, too.

• Create kinetic elements by trapping forms in imaginative ways. For example, when connecting two layers with ball rivets, slide one rivet wire through the interior cutout of a third shape before completing the connection.

• Cut individual lengths of thick wire, ball their ends, and bend them into hanger shapes. Wrap the hanger-shaped base with thinner wire from end to end.

• Weave wire over a hollow form. Position two lightly domed shapes together. Near one end of the hollow form, drill two holes through both layers. Melt a ball on one end of a long piece of thin-gauge wire. Thread the wire through one set of the holes to connect the two domes. Use a loop stitch (see below) to encase the hollow form with woven wire.

• Stitch wire around a drilled circle.

Option A—Drill a series of holes around a copper circle. Bend a heavy-gauge copper wire to fit around the perimeter of the circle. Cut a long length of thinner copper wire, and melt a ball on one end. Thread the wire through a drilled hole in the copper circle. Tightly wrap the thin wire around the thicker wire until you reach another hole drilled in the circle. "Stitch" the thin wire through the hole to secure the thicker wire. Continue this process around the entire edge of the circle. Coil excess heavy-gauge wire in front of the circle for added interest.

Option B—Drill a series of holes around the perimeter of a form. Cut a length of thin wire for each drilled hole. Melt one end of each wire piece. Feed one wire through a hole so that its balled end rests on the front of the form. Stitch the other end of the wire back through the hole several times, anchoring it under the loops on the back of the form.

7. Connect the individual necklace components together. Balance and complete the design by adding additional wire-wrapped dangles in key locations.

8. Use jump rings to attach a handmade toggle and clasp to the ends of the necklace.

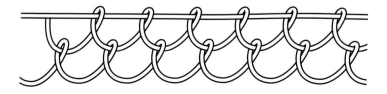

Insight

Looking at the nine items and trying to design with a material constraint was a bit intimidating at first. Once I picked out my wildcard—26-gauge copper wire—I started to feel more comfortable, and my creative juices started to flow. I utilized my textile background to embellish and connect with the thin gauge wire, and thinned the sheet metals down to a workable thickness for me. The circle theme for the necklace was created with the dapping block, the disk cutter, scissors, tube rivets, and balled wire ends for both cold connections and surface interest along with some torch-fired enameling. Once I began working with the materials, I was able to experiment, create, and explore all the endless possibilities. I was challenged to step out of my creative comfort zone.

artist: Mary Hettmansperger

Design Number XIII

Created by **Marcia Macdonald**

unique tab prong setting...
common wildcard with
uncommon beauty...
incredible texture and
meaning

Tools & Materials
Bench tool kit, page 6
Soldering kit, page 6
Checkering file
Anvil or oval mandrel
Old claw hammer with textured face*
Craft knife
Pin catch, stem, and joint
Liver of sulfur
Small chasing tool

*The texture of my hammer face was
achieved by hitting it on sidewalks,
rocks, and old, rusty pitted metal.

Wildcard
Yellow road paint*

*You could also use rusted steel,
wood, plastic, or recycled tin.

From the Box

Method

1. Use a rolling mill to thin the 18-gauge sterling silver sheet to approximately 21 gauge, annealing the metal frequently as you gradually step down its thickness.

2. Use a jeweler's saw to cut two 4 mm strips from silver sheet for the bezel wall. Solder the strips end to end with hard solder. This gives you a strip that is long enough for a large bezel wall.

3. File one long edge of the strip flat with a barrette file. This edge of the bezel will be soldered to the bottom sheet. Use a checkering file to texture what will be the exterior side of the bezel wall. Form the strip into an oval shape. Solder the strip ends together, and pickle the oval shape.

4. Position the oval over an anvil or oval mandrel. Use gentle blows with a plastic hammer to make the oval shape just right.

5. Place a piece of 220-grit sandpaper on a flat surface. Sand the bottom edge of the bezel wall that will be soldered to the flat sheet. This will make soldering much easier.

6. Place the silver oval on top of the yellow road paint. Place the sharp tip of a craft knife inside the silver oval, and score a line in the yellow road paint as close to the inside wall of the bezel as possible. (Fitting the road paint inside the oval before soldering the wall onto the flat sheet is imperative. Otherwise, you won't know what shape to cut.)

7. Cut the road paint with a jeweler's saw, and make sure it fits inside the oval well. (Yes, you can cut paint!) It's better to cut the paint too big than too small. You can always sand or file off excess paint as needed.

8. Use an old claw hammer with textured face to add texture to one surface of the leftover sterling silver sheet. Solder the bezel wall onto the smooth surface of the textured silver sheet. Pickle the bezel.

9. Cut off the excess sterling silver sheet around the bezel wall. File the edges of the silver sheet to desired shape. (I echoed the oval shape and left a tiny, consistent edge of metal around the wall.) Use a rivet hammer to texture the edge of the sheet close to the bezel wall, creating a consistent and considered finish.

10. Create several matching strips from the sterling silver sheet. Solder the strips across the back of the brooch in a "road line" pattern, the kind where passing is allowed. Attach the pin joint and catch to the back of the brooch with easy solder.

11. Use a jeweler's saw to cut six (or more) evenly spaced tabs in the bezel wall. (These are the small "prongs" that will later be pushed down to secure the road paint in the bezel.)

12. Oxidize the brooch in a warm liver of sulfur solution. Clean off excess patina with a green kitchen scrub pad.

13. Attach the pin stem to the joint, and fit it with pliers. Place the road paint into the bezel. Use a burnisher and a small chasing tool to push the tabs over the road paint.

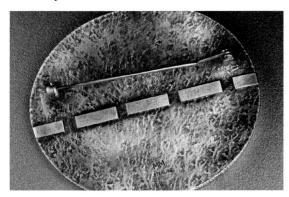

Insight

On Friday, May 22nd, 2009, I finished my last round of chemotherapy for ovarian cancer. A week later I went into the studio for the first time in several months. After the endless medical regime and scheduling I'd endured, I enthusiastically signed on for the challenge with the hope that it would provide a pleasant re-entry into my studio. I knew that I'd benefit from having a "project" to sink my teeth into and the creative space to explore a design challenge that was given to me rather than self imposed.

As the project is about the creative process, I feared that having been out of the studio for so many months I might be facing my own "blank canvas" issues. A fear of the unknown always hits when I have been away from my studio and my tools. Generally all it takes is some time, some good music, some thoughtful inward reflection, and things generally start to flow… but this time seemed different somehow. Would I even want to create? What is meaningful in my life? What can I do that brings me joy and is it making work? What will my work be about now?

When I got the box of materials, I was excited and a bit anxious. But I opened it up and enjoyed looking at all the materials. I also loved the packaging… so clever! While not all of the materials spoke to me, I knew that if I sat with them for a while an idea would come. And an idea did come and then I couldn't wait to get to work.

Simple seems more to me right now and so I chose to use only a couple of the materials and a wildcard—a piece of yellow road paint. I feel I'm on a new path, maybe with old techniques and old familiar tools, but a new path nonetheless. On this road of life you have to give some things a pass, and move on. I enjoy making patterns on the back of my jewelry that reflect something about the piece or to help tell its story. The pattern is a hidden surprise that only the wearer knows.

artist: Marcia Macdonald

Created by **Marlene True**

Design Number XIV

> **"It's a bit like taking a road trip with a destination in mind but stopping and taking detours of interest along the way."**

exquisite construction…

colored tin pops boldly…

found object is integrated seamlessly

Tools & Materials

Bench tool kit, page 6

Soldering kit, page 6

Photocopied design templates, page 125

Steel wire mesh

Rubber cement

Split mandrel

Commercial pinback

Liver of sulfur

Paste wax

200-grit sandpaper

Tin snip, small

Cyanoacrylate glue

Saw blades, 6/0

Pickle for iron wire, 50/50 vinegar and peroxide

Red enamel paint

Wildcard

Tin can

Method

Making the Back Layer of the Brooch

1. Using a jeweler's saw, cut two pieces of copper sheet, each about 1 mm larger than the perimeter of the design. Using a rolling mill, roll one of the 18-gauge copper sheets down to 20 gauge.

2. Sandwich a piece of steel wire mesh between the two copper sheets. Roll this stack through the rolling mill to create a texture that will show on the back of the brooch.

3. Affix the design template for the back of the brooch to the thinner copper sheet with rubber cement, and saw out the metal. File the edges smooth. Load a split mandrel with 400-grit sandpaper, and glide over all edges until smooth. Use 400-grit paper to sand the back and front surfaces.

4. Solder the pin findings to the textured side of the thin copper sheet. Wash the copper with soapy water. Dip the piece into a liver of sulfur solution, and then go over the entire surface with a soft brass brush. Repeat until you're satisfied with the patina. Apply paste wax to the copper, buff it with a soft cloth, and set the back of the brooch aside.

Making the Silver Frame

1. Use a rolling mill to thin the sterling silver sheet to 20 gauge. Affix the template for the exterior frame to the silver sheet with rubber cement. Saw out the frame, and pierce out its interior. File and sand the silver frame.

2. Using a rolling mill, roll the remaining 20-gauge sterling silver sheet, thinning it to 24 gauge (the same thickness as the wire mesh). Affix the template for the interior frame to

From the Box

the 24-gauge silver sheet. Saw out the frame, and pierce out its interior. File and sand the interior frame.

3. Place the 20-gauge, exterior frame facedown on a soldering screen. Flux the back of the frame. Flux the 24-gauge interior frame, and place it on the exterior frame with the fluxed sides touching. Apply a soft bushy torch flame to the sterling silver to dry the flux. When the flux appears glassy, turn off the torch. Dip pieces of medium solder in flux, and place them around the perimeter at 1 cm intervals. Evenly heat the entire piece until the solder flows all the way around the frame. Pickle the metal. Saw off the excess silver, and file and sand the frame. Using 200-grit sandpaper, sand the top surface of the sterling silver in a circular motion until you create an even surface texture. Set the frame aside.

Making the Pearl Cups

1. Using a disk cutter or jeweler's saw, cut a 6.6 mm circle and 7.9 mm circle from the remaining 24-gauge sterling silver. Using a dapping block, dap the silver circles to create cups to hold the pearls.

2. Sand the open side of the cups on 400-grit sandpaper until the surface is flat. Turn the cups over and sand the bottom side until there is a flat surface that will allow the cup to sit flush. Using a 0.84 mm bit, drill a centered hole in the bottom of each pearl cup. Using a larger bit, such as a 1.61 mm, gently bevel each drilled hole by hand.

3. Position the pearl cups on the sterling silver frame with the larger cup on the right side, and mark their locations. Center punch and drill at each marked point with a 0.84 mm bit. Flux the bottom of the silver cups and the sterling frame, and place the cups on the frame.

4. Cut two pieces of sterling silver wire, each approximately 1 inch (2.5 cm) long. Flux one end of each wire, and feed them through the cups and the holes in the frame. Place one piece of easy solder under each cup. Evenly heat the metal to flow the solder. Run a burnisher along the inside and outside edges of the frame to give it a bright shine.

Making & Installing the Mesh

1. Place the photocopied mesh template on top of the fine silver mesh. Securely hold the pattern in place as you trace it onto the mesh with a thick black permanent marker. Using a tin snip, cut along the inside edge

of the marked line—be generous, you can always trim a little more off for a perfect fit.

2. Place the mesh inside the frame, and trim to fit. Place a very small amount of glue in two opposite corners, and set aside. (The adhesive is only a temporary means of holding the screen in place. The glue prevents the screen from falling out when being riveted later.)

Riveting the Frame to the Back of the Brooch

1. Mark all four corners of the silver frame. Center punch and drill each mark with a 0.84 mm bit. Bevel the holes by hand with a larger bit. Position the silver frame over the copper back. Mark one hole through the frame and onto the copper. Center punch and drill one hole in the copper. Using sterling silver wire, rivet the sterling frame to the copper in one corner.

2. Reposition the silver frame on the copper back, and hold the pieces firmly in place. At the corner across from the first rivet, drill a hole through the copper. Set the rivet through this hole, and then drill and rivet the remaining two holes. If needed, add additional rivets to keep the silver frame flush with the copper back.

Creating the Rabbit

1. Use rubber cement to adhere the photocopied rabbit template to the remaining 24-gauge sterling silver sheet. Saw, file, and sand the rabbit shape. Using medium solder, solder a copper washer to the back of the sterling silver rabbit. Using a 0.84 mm bit, drill three equidistant holes through the washer and the rabbit. Bevel each hole by hand with a larger drill bit.

2. Cut three 1-inch (2.5 cm) lengths of sterling silver wire. Position the silver rabbit over the frame and screen, and firmly hold the pieces together. Drill through one of the existing holes in the rabbit straight through the copper back. Feed one of the sterling silver wires through the rabbit and the copper to hold the pieces in place while drilling the next two holes. Drill through a second hole in the rabbit and through the copper back. Place a wire in the hole. Finally, drill through the third rabbit hole.

3. Remove the silver rabbit and the wires from the brooch. Place the rabbit on a flat soldering surface with the copper washer facing up. Using easy solder, solder the three wires in place.

4. Using a tin snip, carefully cut down the side and around the bottom of a painted tin can. Use a mallet to flatten the sheet. Cut out a 3-inch-square (7.6 cm) section of the tin. Use rubber cement to adhere the smaller rabbit template over the desired section of the tin. Using a 6/0 blade, carefully saw out the rabbit.

5. Center punch and drill holes around the perimeter of the tin rabbit, just enough to hold it in place. Place the tin rabbit over the silver rabbit. Mark, center punch, and drill one hole. Rivet the tin rabbit to the silver rabbit with sterling silver wire. Repeat this process until riveting is complete. Straighten the wires on the back of the silver rabbit, and carefully feed these through the holes drilled through the copper back. Trim the wires, and rivet the rabbit to the brooch.

Attaching the Red X & the Pearls

1. Saw a small X shape out of a piece of tin. Sand the back of the tin, apply flux, and then solder a 1-inch (2.5 cm) piece of sterling silver wire to the back. Pickle the X shape in a bath of 50/50 vinegar and peroxide. Sand the surface of the X, and paint it with red enamel paint.

2. Drill a hole through the copper back where the X will be placed. Cut a 1 to 1.5 mm piece of sterling silver tubing, and feed this tube over the sterling wire on the X. Feed the wire through the hole in the brooch, and trim and rivet it.

3. Trim the wires in the pearl cups to 2.5 mm long. Test the pearls to make sure they slide all the way down and seat in the cups. Remove the pearls, place a dot of glue on the post, and slide the pearl back down the wire. Let dry.

Insight

While working, ideas from one piece often feed the next. I had just finished working on a narrative brooch, which had a negative space cut out forming a rabbit silhouette. The remaining positive shape and the wire mesh—which I was attracted to immediately—began to affect my ideas for this project. However, sketching out a complete design for this project was a bit of a challenge for me. In my usual process of making a piece, I like to remain open to ideas as they come. It's a bit like taking a road trip with a destination in mind but stopping and taking detours of interest along the way.

artist: Marlene True

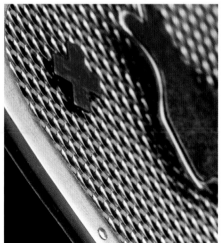

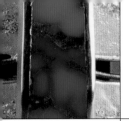

Created by **Ross Coppelman**
Design Number XV

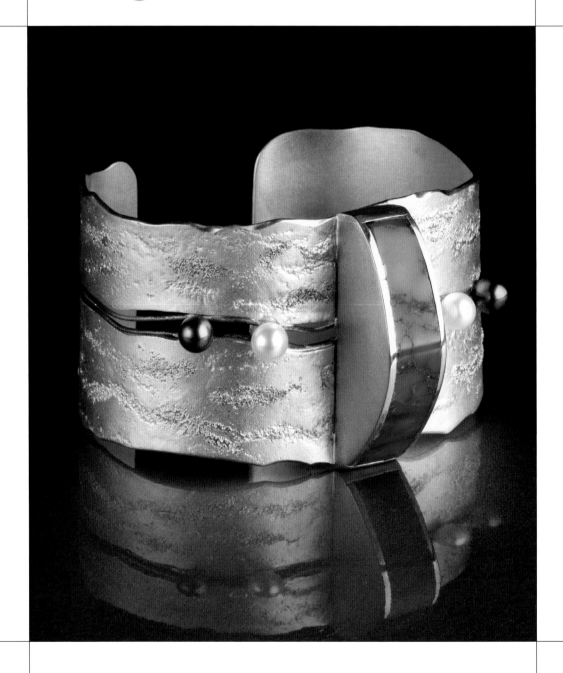

inventive wire inlay...
superior craftsmanship...
a masterful setting for an
exquisite stone...

Materials & Tools

Bench tool kit, page 6
Soldering kit, page 6
Small paintbrush or metal pick
    (optional)
14-gauge wire
Draw plate
Polishing compounds,
    Tripoli and red rouge
Muslin buffing wheel
Mini sandblasting unit
Epoxy

Wildcard

Turquoise

Method

1. Cut the sterling silver sheet into two 1½ x 3-inch (3.8 x 7.6 cm) pieces. On each piece, measure and mark a line that is 3 mm inside one end. On the opposite end of each piece, measure and mark a line that is 2.5 cm away from the end.

2. On both silver pieces, draw a curving channel that is approximately 3 mm wide and travels from one marked line to the other. Drill a hole in the center of each channel, and saw out the shapes.

3. Arrange the silver pieces so the ends where the channels start closest to the edge meet. Solder the two pieces together with hard silver solder. Using a jeweler's saw, create organic edges around the entire silver sheet.

4. Using a coarse file, file some copper sheet to a grainy dust. File some hard silver solder to the same consistency. Mix the filings in a ratio of 6 to 8 parts copper to 1 part silver solder.

5. Randomly scatter the copper/solder mixture on the surface of the silver sheet. Use a small paintbrush or a metal pick to create patterns, if desired. Once pleased with the arrangement, heat the entire sheet until the solder melts.

6. Cut four copper wires that are slightly longer than the curving channels. Fit two wires inside each channel, bending their shape to echo the

From the Box

"Before I knew what the exact materials were going to be, I decided that I wanted to make the biggest piece possible out of sterling."

curves of the cutout design. Snip off any excess wire. Spot solder the ends of the wires to the ends of the channels. Spot solder the wires to the sides of the channels at two or three more points.

7. Using a rawhide hammer, shape the bracelet around a bracelet mandrel. Stand a steel bench block on edge. Place the center of the bracelet on top of the block. Flatten the center section of the bracelet—the area that lies between the two channels—until it is approximately 1 cm wide.

8. To make the pegs for the pearls, cut four 1 cm pieces of 14-gauge sterling silver wire. Melt one end of each wire into a ball. Locate a hole on a draw plate that is slightly larger than 14 gauge. One at a time, feed a wire through the flat surface of the draw plate and tap the balled end of the wire flat with a ball peen hammer. This creates a nail-like head on the wires.

9. Drill halfway into the pearls with a 1.78 mm bit so that the 14-gauge wire will fit snugly into the holes.

10. Measure the turquoise at its highest point. Add 1 mm to this measurement. Measure the long and short sides of the stone. Add 6 mm to the length of one long side and one short side combined. Cut two strips from the copper sheet to these measurements.

11. Refer to the figure on page 126 to determine where your bezel strips need to bend at a right angle. Mark this point on the strips. Use a triangular needle file to score a perpendicular groove one-third to one-half of the way through the copper sheet. Using flat-nose pliers, bend the right angle in the sheet.

12. Place the long side of one bent strip flat on your work surface. Nestle the stone onto the corner of the strip. Place the second strip on top of the stone. Trim both ends of the second strip until you've created a bezel that is barely larger than the stone. Solder the joints of the bezel, and trim off excess with saw and files.

13. Solder the bottom of the bezel to a piece of copper sheet. Cut the copper sheet slightly longer

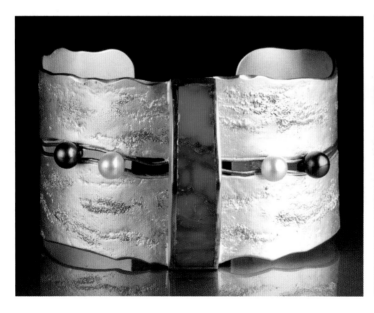

than the bezel. Trim the excess copper from around the bottom of the bezel. Make the top edge of the bezel flush to the stone. Sand and polish all joints.

14. To attach the bezel to the bracelet, flow medium solder onto the bottom of the bezel. Place the bezel on the flat area at the top of the bracelet. Slowly heat the entire piece from above and below until the bezel solders onto the bracelet.

15. Snugly wedge two pearl pegs between the copper wires in each channel. Adjust the spacing of the pegs so they are equidistant on both sides of the bezel. Solder the pegs in place with easy solder. Cut the pegs so the pearls will be flush to the surface of the bracelet.

16. Polish all edges of the bracelet with Tripoli compound on a felt wheel, followed by a muslin buff on all surfaces. Sandblast the entire piece with a mini sandblasting unit. Lightly rouge the entire piece.

17. Epoxy the pearls into place. Epoxy and/or bezel set the turquoise into the setting.

Insight

The project was definitely challenging on many fronts. It reminded me of my feelings about my dog after a skunk sprayed him. I both loved him and wanted to get as far away as I could. Part of me embraced this challenge and part of me wanted to totally avoid it. The materials presented in the box did not inspire any special desire or spark—too much black and grey. My normal material choice is high karat gold, which has a color that moves me. That said, there were lots of interesting items in the box—the mesh, the cord, the tubing. Because no distinct designs arose from my encounter with the elements in the box, I decided to take another approach. How could I use any of these items in some untraditional way? That is when I conceived of using copper filings to make patterns on a silver surface, although this process required some trial and error. I was hoping the randomness of the copper patterning would give the bracelet a spontaneity.

If I hadn't committed to this design in my proposal, I would have definitely changed it during the fabrication process. I hardly ever have a piece fully visualized before I begin making it, and even when I do, it morphs. In my work, the random, unexpected element frequently pops up and leads me to change course and head off into new directions. For me, that is the most exciting part of the creative process.

artist: Ross Coppelman

Created by **Candie Cooper**

Design Number XVI

a single swatch of felt...
natural and feminine...
texture, color, and depth
delicately framed

Materials & Tools

Photocopied design template,
    page 127
Bench tool kit, page 6
Grinding wheel
Cross peen hammer
Liver of sulfur
Bubble wrap
Needle
Multi-purpose epoxy

Wildcard

Burgundy merino wool &
    sewing threads

From the Box

Method

Preparing the Metal Elements

1. Make 22 jump rings out of the 20-gauge copper wire, each 8 mm in diameter. Make two more copper jump rings, each 6 mm in diameter.

2. Transfer the photocopied templates onto the sheet metal. Use the sterling silver sheet for the leaf links and round frame (it's a tight squeeze, but you can do it!), and the copper sheet for the round base. Saw out the pieces.

3. Mark and drill seven centered and evenly spaced holes around the round frame with a 1.6 mm bit (see template for placement). Position the round frame on top of the copper base, and carefully drill through the existing holes so the holes in the sheet line up perfectly for riveting later. Texture the round frame with a grinding wheel.

4. Drill the holes in the leafy links with a 0.89 mm bit. File and sand the links and copper base piece.

5. Lay the round frame on top of the silver mesh, and trim around the excess mesh with snips. Tape the two pieces together, and drill back through the holes in the frame to remove the wires from the mesh, making room for the tube rivets.

6. Lay the copper base on the steel bench block, and hammer around its edge with a cross peen hammer.

7. Oxidize the leaf links, the copper base, and the round silver frame in a liver of sulfur solution. Rub the round silver frame with pumice to remove some of the patina. Finish all oxidized metal parts with a brass brush and dish soap.

Creating & Attaching the Wool Elements

1. To create the wool layer that goes under the mesh, first tear off a few very thin wisps of wool. Place a piece of bubble wrap on your work surface with the bubble side facing up. Lay two wisps of wool side by side on the bubble wrap. Lay two more wisps of wool on top of and perpendicular to the first pair. Pour a tablespoon (15 mL) or so of warm water and a drop of dish soap onto the wool. Place a second piece of bubble wrap on top of the wet wool. Rub the top of the bubble wrap for approximately five minutes. Check to see if the fabric is intact—if not, keep agitating. If it is intact, rinse the fabric in cold water and let it dry. The final piece of wool should be very thin.

2. Lay the mesh on top of the finished fabric, and trim away the excess wool. Do not discard the wool scraps. Cut another piece of wool to fit inside an 8 mm copper jump ring.

3. Using the project photo as a guide, stitch the jump ring to the mesh with the copper and mauve threads. Tuck the small circle of wool inside the 8 mm copper jump ring, and secure it with a French knot in the center.

4. Stitch a ½-inch (1.3 cm) copper washer to the screen with burgundy and silver threads. Using copper and mauve threads, add a French knot at the end of each stitch around the washer.

5. Stack the pieces in the following order, bottom to top: copper base sheet, wool and screen, and round silver frame. Based on the depth of this stack, cut seven pieces of sterling silver tubing to use as rivets. Tube rivet the stack.

Embellishing the Leaf Links

1. Texture each leaf link with the grinding wheel attachment. Dome each of the links in a shallow cavity on the dapping block.

2. Cut six pieces of silver wire, each 1 inch (2.5 cm) long. Melt one end of each wire into a ball.

3. Cut three 1.1 cm circles from the leftover silver mesh. Dome each mesh circle in a fairly deep cavity in the steel dapping block. Oxidize the mesh domes in a liver of sulfur solution.

4. Fit a small circle of wool fabric into a mesh dome. With the copper and mauve thread, whip-stitch around the edge to connect the two materials. Repeat this step for the remaining mesh domes.

5. Cut three more mesh circles, each 1.3 cm in diameter. These are for the pearl "nets." Dome each mesh circle until it's nearly closed (you may need to trim as you go). Squeeze a white pearl into each "net," and close up the mesh around it.

6. Oxidize the mesh-covered pearls, the balled wires, and the leaf links with a liver of sulfur solution. Rub each of the leaf links with pumice to remove some of the oxidation, and then with a brass brush and dish soap.

7. Thread a balled wire from the back of a leaf link through a drilled hole. Place a mesh-covered pearl onto the wire on the front of the link, and check the fit. Trim the wire as needed so there are no gaps between the elements. Secure the mesh-covered pearls to the ends of the wires with epoxy.

Making the Chain

1. Select two ⁷⁄₁₆-inch (1.1 cm) copper washers, four ⁵⁄₁₆-inch (8 mm) copper washers, and two ⅜-inch (1 cm) copper washers to use for the chain. One at a time, place the two ⁷⁄₁₆-inch (1.1 cm) copper washers on the steel bench block, and hammer one side with a cross peen hammer to create a ray-like texture. Hammer both of the ⅜-inch (1 cm) washers to create the same effect. Use the flat face of a chasing hammer to flatten six of the 8 mm copper jump rings.

2. For the clasp, saw a 0.2 x 3.2 cm strip out of the copper sheet. File and sand the cut edges. Using round-nose pliers, bend the strip into a hook. Hammer the edges of the hook with a cross peen hammer.

3. Draw a leaf shape on the leftover silver sheet. Saw and pierce out the leaf form, and then texture it with a grinding wheel.

4. Oxidize all the washers, jump rings, and clasp pieces in a liver of sulfur solution. Rub the leaf-shaped clasp element with pumice. Use a brass brush with dish soap to finish all of the chain elements.

5. Create one side of the chain by linking the elements in the following order:

1 hammered $\frac{7}{16}$- inch (1.1 cm) copper washer

1 plain 8 mm jump ring, 1 flattened 8 mm jump ring, 1 plain 8 mm jump ring

1 plain $\frac{5}{16}$-inch (8 mm) copper washer

1 plain 8 mm jump ring, one flattened 8 mm jump ring, one plain 8 mm jump ring

1 hammered $\frac{3}{8}$-inch (1 cm) copper washer

1 plain 8 mm jump ring, one flattened 8 mm jump ring, one plain 8 mm jump ring

1 plain $\frac{5}{16}$-inch (8 mm) copper

washer

1 plain 8 mm jump ring

Repeat this step to create the second side of the chain.

6. Connect one leaf link to each side of the central flower element with a 6 mm copper jump ring. Connect a leaf link to each of the largest hammered washers with an 8 mm jump ring. Connect one clasp element to the plain 8 mm jump ring on each end of the chain.

Insight

One of the things I love most about designing is the problem solving it involves, so the jewelry challenge was right up my alley. The challenge forced me to try things that I normally wouldn't have tried. I chose fiber as my wildcard because I use a lot of wool in my work, and I'm intrigued with pairing soft wool and hard, cold metal. One thing that surprised me was that I found a certain freedom within the constraints of the materials. In my studio, I have endless options for materials, which means a lot of decision-making—although I have to admit I was nervous when I opened the box and saw all that copper! I used liver of sulphur to oxidize it and loved the rosy glow after tumbling.

artist: Candie Cooper

Design Number XVII
Created by **Annie Chau**

alternative stone setting...captures the essence of pearls...vibrant motion and sound

Tools & Materials

Bench tool kit, page 6
Soldering kit, page 6
Ring mandrel
Liver of sulfur
Bezel setting tools

Wildcard

Scalloped sterling silver
    bezel wire

From the Box

Method

1. Use dapping tools to dap the sterling silver mesh into the desired dome size. Trim away any excess mesh. Lightly run the edges of the mesh dome over sandpaper to ensure that the edges are level and will sit flush in the bezel setting.

2. Measure and cut the scalloped bezel wire to fit snuggly around the mesh dome. Solder the ends of the bezel wire together. Pickle the soldered piece. Check that the finished bezel fits snuggly over the dome, and adjust as needed.

3. Solder the finished bezel to the sterling silver sheet. Pickle the soldered piece.

4. Trim away the excess sterling silver sheet around the bezel with a jeweler's saw. Refine the cut edge with files and sandpaper until the silver sheet is flush with the exterior wall of the bezel wire.

5. Determine the desired size of your ring. Using the ring mandrel and a mallet, shape the sterling silver tubing to form the band. Solder the band onto the completed bezel setting.

6. Oxidize the ring and mesh dome with a liver of sulfur solution.

7. Place the pearls into the bezel setting. Position the mesh dome over the pearls and inside the bezel setting. Securely set the mesh dome.

Insight

The challenge was a lot harder than I thought it would be. I had an immediate desire to depart from my usual aesthetic while using as many of the materials provided as possible, but this became quite difficult as I've never used some of the ingredients before, like the mesh and the pearls. I really enjoyed the challenge, though, because I worked with materials in a way I would not have conventionally. For example, I used tubing to make the ring shank. I had a great time!

artist: Annie Chau

Created by **Deb Karash**

Design Number XVIII

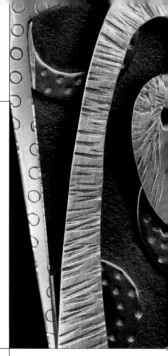

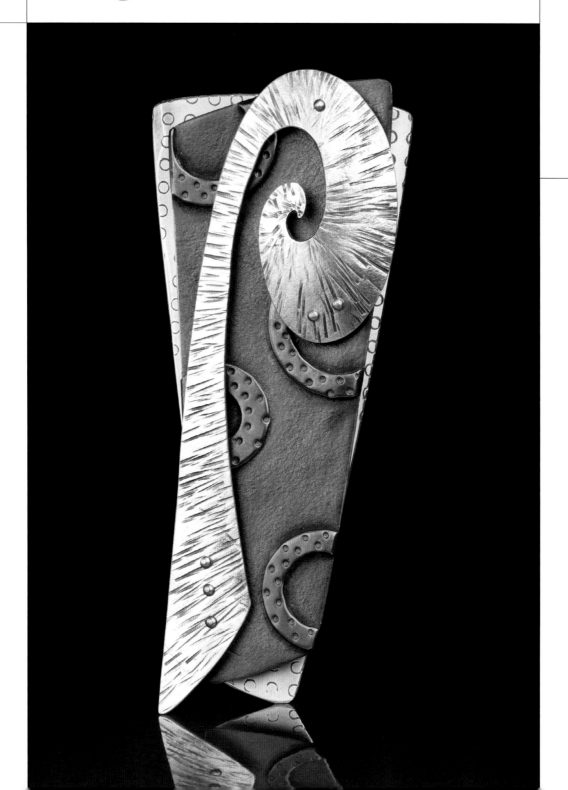

depth of textures...bail for added versatility...construction creates dimension...

Materials & Tools

Photocopied design templates, page 126
Soldering kit, page 6
Bench tool kit, page 6
2 texture sheets for use with rolling mill*
Texturing hammer**
Forming stake
Ring mandrel (optional)
Pin stem and catch
Liver of sulfur
Wax sealant
Abrasive wheel for the buffer, fine
Radial bristle disk for the buffer, fine
Hammer handpiece with round bit
   (optional)

For this project, the texture on the silver sheet came from a piece of brass with an etched pattern of small circles. The texture on the copper sheet came from a piece of paper.

**For this project, the designer ground down the face of an inexpensive hammer, giving it a sharp edge.*

Wildcard

6 brass escutcheon pins*, 20 gauge

Escutcheon pins feature a smooth shank with a half-round head. Typically stouter than wire nails, they have many functional and decorative applications.

From the Box

Method

Creating the Brooch Layers

1. Sketch a three-layer design for your brooch. The front and back layers will be made from sterling silver, and the middle layer will be made from copper. Photocopy the sketch to create a template for each layer or use the templates on page 126.

2. Anneal the copper and silver sheets. Roll each metal sheet through the rolling mill to achieve a thickness of 22 gauge. On the last pass through the mill, roll texture onto the sterling silver sheet and onto the copper sheet.

3. Trace the outline for the back layer onto the textured sterling silver sheet. Cut out this shape with a jeweler's saw. Trace the outline for the middle layer onto the textured copper sheet. Cut out this shape with a jeweler's saw.

4. Trace the outline for the front layer on the sterling silver sheet. Using a texture hammer, hammer a pattern into the metal. Cut out the front layer of sterling silver with a jeweler's saw.

Expert Tip: Hammering the texture before cutting out the front layer keeps the shape from becoming distorted.

---

5. Select four copper washers and sand their backs. Determine the placement of the washers on the copper layer. (If half or more of the washer hangs over the edge of the copper layer, support it with a piece of copper that is also 22 gauge.) Solder the washers to the copper layer in the

"I feel that even though I'm known for doing color, it's the structure and textures in my pieces that make them work."

desired pattern. (I used paste solder, which saves time and has a sticky property that keeps the components in place.)

6. Trim the overhanging washers. Use a fine-point permanent marker to draw a pattern of dots onto washers. Using a punch and hammer, stamp the dot pattern into the washers.

Expert Tip: Brace the hand holding the punch so the tool does not drift. Very little force is needed when stamping. It's best to do a test on scrap metal before stamping onto the brooch component.

---

7. File all edges of the front, middle, and back layers of the brooch. Bevel the edges of the copper washers on the middle layer.

Preparing for Connection

1. Mark the placement of the rivets on the top sterling silver layer. Drill each marked point with an 0.89 mm bit.

2. Position the front layer of the brooch on top of the middle layer, and redrill through one hole made in step 1. Temporarily place a rivet into

that hole. Redrill and place a temporary rivet in one more hole, and then drill all remaining holes from the front layer through the middle layer.

3. Position the middle layer of the brooch on top of the back layer. Drill through and place temporary rivets in two holes, and then drill all remaining holes.

4. On the back of the bottom layer, use a larger drill bit to bevel the rivet holes. This step allows the rivets to be flush with the surface and makes for a stronger bond.

5. Place the front layer of the brooch on a forming stake. Hammer the layer with a leather mallet to dome the metal. Roll the edges of the metal by hammering the vertical edges over a stake or ring mandrel with a leather mallet.

6. Solder the pin stem and catch onto the back layer of the brooch. (Pin findings should always be positioned in the top third of the brooch, and the joint should be angled so that the stem will rest just above the catch when open. Make sure the catch is in the semi-open position, with the "rabbit ears" positioned at the top.)

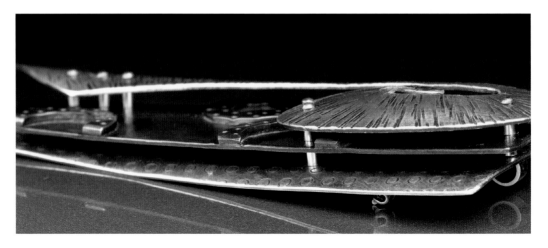

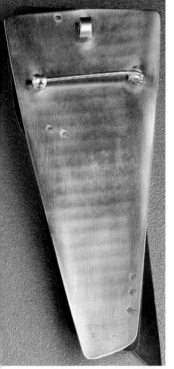

Finishing & Connecting

1. Color all three metal layers with a liver of sulfur solution. Brush the copper layer with a wire brush, and then coat it with a wax sealant. Buff the back layer of the brooch with a fine abrasive wheel. Burnish its edges with a steel burnisher, and then coat it with a wax sealant. Buff the front layer with a fine radial bristle disk and coat it with a wax sealant.

2. Cut six pieces of tubing, each 2 mm long. Cut six more pieces of tubing, each 3 mm long.

3. Feed the 20-gauge escutcheon pins through the holes in the top layer of the brooch. Place a drop of a strong adhesive on each pin where it exits the hole. Slide a piece of tubing that is 3 mm long onto each pin.

4. Feed the escutcheon pins through the copper layer of the brooch. Place a drop of a strong adhesive on each pin where it exits the hole. Slide a piece of tubing that is 2 mm long onto each pin.

5. Feed the escutcheon pins through the back layer of the brooch, and turn the piece over onto a steel bench block. Cut the pins flush with the back layer, and hammer them closed. (I use a hammer handpiece with a round bit that I have shaped slightly larger than the rivet.)

6. Place the pin stem into the hinge, and rivet it. Clean up the back of the brooch with the fine abrasive wheel, and apply a wax sealant.

Insight

When I got the invitation, I was intrigued by the challenge of working with a fixed set of materials that were not necessarily the materials I am used to working with. When I got the materials, I unpacked them and just sat with them for a while. They were all so tempting, but I didn't want to use too many materials just because they were there. I wanted to keep it simple but interesting, but I also wanted my project to look like my work. I had a hard time choosing my wildcard. I ended up using the rivets, because I feel that even though I'm known for doing color, it's the structure and textures in my pieces that make them work. I thought that I might be inspired to carry over something from this project into my own work, and in fact, I did do a number of pieces with a similar spiral form.

artist: Deb Karash

Created by **Colleen Baran**

Design Number XIX

metal in liquid movement...
graceful curves...adaptable
in size and complexity

Tools & Materials

Standard sheets of paper,
  for pattern organization (optional)
Sheet of cardboard or tray (optional)
Bench tool kit, page 6
Small bracelet mandrel or mandrel
  in desired hoop size
Large circle template with
  1⅝-inch (4.1 cm) diameter
Soldering kit, page 6
Disk cutting set (optional)
Small circle template
  with 4.5 mm diameter
Earring posts and backings
Pearl cement

Wildcard

Sterling silver wire, 18 gauge,
36 to 48 inches (91.4 to 121.9 cm)

Note from the Designer

The earrings feature a number of little twiggy bits that all look rather similar when bundled. I used a couple sheets of paper to label the parts needed and to organize them into separate rows for each earring. This method provided me with a sense of my progress, tracked uniformity, and made the process feel pleasantly organized.

Method

Forming the Individual Wires

1. Cut the 18-gauge and 20-gauge sterling silver wires in half, and separate them. Cut and reserve two 1-inch (2.5 cm) pieces of 20-gauge silver wire to use later for pearl posts.

2. Wrap each wire around a small bracelet mandrel to form coils that are 1⅝ inches (4.1 cm) in diameter. Keep the springiness of the wire in mind in order to make coils of the right diameter. Use the large circle template as needed to reference the size.

3. Cut the coiled wire into the sizes listed below. Use the large circle template as needed for reference. (You can use wire cutters to cut the wire, as the ends will be balled later.) Organize each wire size into a separate group.

From the 18-gauge silver wire coil:
    Two pieces, each 1⅛ circle (Wire A)
    Two pieces, each ¾ circle (Wire B)
    Four pieces, each ½ circle (Wire C)
    Two pieces, each ⅜ circle (Wire D)

From the 20-gauge silver wire coil:
    Two pieces, each ¾ circle
    Two pieces, each ½ circle
    Two pieces, each ¼ circle

From the Box

4. Melt the cut ends of the curved wire pieces into balls.

For the 18-gauge wire (larger balls are better):
    Wires A, B, and D—1.5 to 2 mm
        balls on both ends
    Wire C—1.5 to 2 mm balls on one end,
        2 to 2.5 mm balls on the other

For all 20-gauge wire pieces—1.5 to 2 mm balls on both ends

Constructing the Wire Hoops

(Rather then saying 'repeat' after each step, the designer details how to make one hoop. For ease and for symmetry's sake, we recommend making both earrings, step by step, at the same time.)

1. Using an "A" length of 18-gauge wire, slide one balled end under the coil to face the other balled wire end. (Rather then forcing the wire, just lightly anneal it and gently move it into place.) Solder the balled end to the coil at the point of intersection. Leave the other balled wire end unattached. (This framework provides a light, two-layer base to work off of. It adds strength and stability and can be adjusted while working but is still held together at one end.)

2. Slide the "B" length of 18-gauge wire between the layers made in step 1, keeping it and all subsequent wires positioned within three-quarters of the full coil. (The remaining one-quarter of the coil will be snipped off later to make room for the ear post.) Fit the new wire in comfortably rather than forcing it, and determine an aesthetically appealing resting place. Rest the wire assembly on the soldering block, and solder one end of the "B" length to the coil.

3. Slide a "C" length of 18-gauge wire between the layers of the coil. Position the end with the large ball on the inside of the hoop, near the center. Place the end with the small ball on the outside of the hoop near the front. Rest the wire assembly on the soldering block, and solder one end of the "C" length to the coil.

4. Continue to add layers of 18-gauge and 20-gauge bent wires to the form, twisting and weaving them in by crossing over and under layers to form the hoop. Leave the bottom of the hoop fairly open so you will later have room for the pearl.

Expert Tip: Periodically polish the wire forms so ultimately you'll have a cleaner finish. Polishing is easier when the wire is exposed, rather than once it is buried, so do it incrementally.

Making the Pad for the Pearl

1. Cut a 1-inch-square (2.5 cm) piece of sterling silver sheet. Using a rolling mill, roll the silver sheet down to approximately 26 gauge. Anneal the rolled silver sheet.

2. Using either a circle punch or a jeweler's saw, cut out two 4.5 mm disks to use as the pads for the pearls. Find the center of each disk with a small circle template, and mark these points with a fine-tip permanent marker. Center punch an indentation at the marked points. Wearing proper safety equipment, drill a 0.5 mm hole at each indentation. Dome the disks in a dapping block to fit the curve of the pearls. Redrill the holes in the domed disks with a 0.8 mm bit so the wire stems will fit snugly inside.

3. Thread a 1-inch (2.5 cm) piece of 20-gauge wire through the hole in the domed disk. Adjust the wire so that 6 mm extends as a post for the pearl and 1.9 cm extends past the pad as a stem. Solder the wire to the pad. Polish the pad.

4. Slide the pad for the pearl between layers in the hoop. Position the pad so it is symmetrical on each hoop. (If asymmetry is preferred, just be sure that the large silver balls that will be added later are balanced in the arrangement.) Once the pads are in a pleasing spot, mark the position with a permanent marker and carefully solder the pad in place. (Leave the protruding bit of wire in place. It will make a convenient handle when soldering on pod balls later.)

Making & Attaching the Silver Balls

1. Use the leftover sterling silver sheet to make large silver balls that complement the size of the pearls. (A large, 4.8 mm ball will weigh approximately 0.5 grams, a 4 mm ball approximately 0.4 grams, and a 3 mm ball approximately 0.2 grams.) Put on soldering

safety glasses, and place the scrap sheet on a charcoal block. Melt two pairs of balls, one pair that is approximately 3.5 mm in diameter and one pair that is approximately 4.5 mm in diameter.

2. Determine where to place the silver balls on the hoops, keeping in mind where the pearl will eventually sit. Clamp the excess wire protruding from the pearl pad in a pair of interlocking tweezers so the hoop stands vertically upright. Solder a bit of easy solder to the underside of the silver ball. Balance the silver ball in position on the hoop. Solder the ball to the hoop evenly but delicately so as not to melt the surrounding wires. Repeat this process to attach the remaining silver balls.

Finishing the Earrings

1. Carefully sweat solder the wires together at the points where they touch. (Following the natural shape of the interwoven wires will maintain fluidity in the hoops, whereas forcing the wires together will cause a coarseness in the design. Sweat soldering in key points provides strength and stability and allows light and delicate pieces added sturdiness.) Watch for the flash of solder, drawing it along the wires where they touch, then quickly withdraw the solder and flame. Test for weak and unattached areas and solder these, but let the woven wires remain otherwise open.

2. Cut off the quarter of the circle at the top of the hoop that was providing support as the earrings were constructed. Ball the newly cut wire ends. Solder an earring post onto each hoop, and work harden the posts by gently twisting the metal with flat pliers. Trim the wire that protrudes from the pearl pad, and ball the cut end. Pickle, rinse, and dry the hoops.

3. Lightly polish the hoops with rubber wheels. If needed, clean up bits of lightly melted wire and smooth the balls, wire ends, and any forming marks.

4. Fully polish the hoops with peach and green bristle wheels. (Bristle wheels can easily slide inside the wire layers. The designer left a bit of the fine white silver on the hoops to subtly set off the pearl.) Adhere the pearl to the stem on top of the pad with pearl cement, and let dry.

Insight

When I received my box of materials, I was rather giddy with anticipation. But despite this eagerness, I let my ideas incubate. Usually I work directly with the materials and let the ideas flow as I work, inspired by the actual process of making. Here I chose to vary my method by letting the ideas develop on paper first, largely because this was the first multi-technique project I'd written and it was challenging in a new way.

I made regular "book project" trips to cafes to draw. Fueled by strong spicy tea and muffins, I mulled over ideas. Looking at the thin wire, I was inspired by the thought of growth, leafy tendrils, grassy bits, and pods of silver.

One of my objectives was to make earrings that were both essentially "me" and yet universal—that could easily be personalized with slight alterations like using thicker or thinner wire, looser or tighter patterns, larger or smaller balls, and more or less overlapping pieces.

artist: Colleen Baran

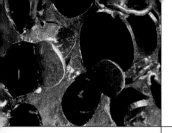

Design Number XX
Created by **Biba Schutz**

texture abounds...
dimension from flat
sheet...organic yet
intentional

Materials & Tools

Tools for texturing metal
Photocopied design
    template, page 125
Bench tool kit, page 6
Soldering kit, page 6

Wildcard

Stainless-steel wire for
    pin stem, 20 gauge

From the Box

Method

1. Texture the surface of the copper sheet as desired. Transfer the photocopied template onto the copper sheet. Use a jeweler's saw to cut out the transferred shape.

2. Using the photo as a guide, create a piercing pattern on the back of the copper shape. Pierce and saw out the design.

3. Score the fold lines on the copper shape, and then fold the box. Fold up all pierced elements.

4. Drill several pairs of holes on the front of the brooch between the pierced elements. Cut a length of copper wire for each pair of drilled holes. Melt a ball on one end of each wire length.

5. From the back of the brooch, thread a balled wire through a drilled hole, bend it down through its neighboring hole, and melt a ball in the second wire end. Repeat this step to make a wire loop in each pair of drilled holes.

6. Cut a ¾-inch (1.9 cm) length of sterling silver tubing. Solder this tube to the back of the brooch on the edge that is directly across from the clasp. Fold up the metal for the clasp and saw out its interior form.

7. Use a torch to apply a heat patina to the copper brooch.

8. To make the pin stem, insert the stainless steel wire into the tube soldered onto the back of the brooch. Form the wire into a U shape, insert it into the catch, cut off any excess wire, and finish the tips.

Insight

My approach to this challenge began with a single idea: use simple tools and one material to create something unique. While developing the project, I knew I wanted to start with a creative interpretation of a very basic idea; I chose the cardboard box lid. I also wanted to make a piece that encouraged an association of memory and that would, at the same time, inspire the maker to use the idea, but with their own interpretation.

artist: Biba Schutz

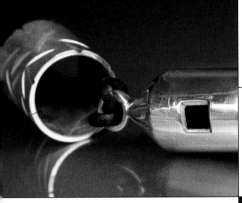

Created by **Tim McCreight**

Design Number XXI

well-engineered...

skilled use of file for

decorative purposes...

handmade accents

underscore

impeccable design

Tools & Materials

Bench tool kit, page 6
Soldering kit, page 6
Ring-forming pliers
Escapement files
Epoxy

Wildcard

None

Method

Making the Interior Cylinder

1. Measure and mark a 2 x 5 cm rectangle on the sterling silver sheet. (This rectangle will become the inner cylinder of the locket.) Neatly saw out the rectangle.

2. Mark an opening, or "window," of any shape on the silver rectangle. (The opening in this project is a rectangle, positioned vertically.) Drill a hole inside the marked opening, then pierce it out with a jeweler's saw. Clean the cut edges with small files.

3. To bend the silver strip into a cylinder, hold one end in ring-forming pliers. Bend the opposite end up to form a half cylinder. Repeat the process from the other end, bringing the two ends as close together as possible. Press the ends together, using a mallet if necessary.

4. Clean up the joint by passing a saw blade through it, perhaps several times, until the edges of the seam meet perfectly. Solder the joint closed. True up the cylinder on whatever rods are handy and appropriate.

5. Following the instructions in the sidebar at right, lay out a cone shape on paper. Transfer this design onto the sterling sheet.

Making a Cone Pattern

1. Draw an accurate side view of the cone.

2. Extend the sides to meet at D.

3. Set a compass with radius BD and scribe an arc.

4. Multiply AB times pi (3.14) and mark this distance along the arc BC.

5. Connect DC. The shaded portion is the pattern.

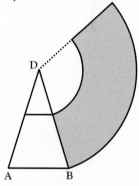

From the Box

"In the end, I decided to take a minimalist approach and confine myself to a single material."

Expert Tip: The 18-gauge thickness of the sterling silver sheet will come in handy later when filing a dimensional pattern, but this thickness makes bending the top of the cone very difficult. A good solution is to planish the sterling silver, thinning the area that will be the top of the cone.

6. Saw out the silver arc. To bend it into a cone shape, start at the ends and use ring-forming pliers as described in step 3. Clean up the joint, and solder the cone closed.

7. File the bottom edge of the cone to make it flat and symmetrical. Solder the cone onto the top of the cylinder.

8. Draw a series of evenly spaced lines on the cone with a permanent marker. Lightly notch each line with a saw. Starting with a triangular file, file a series of grooves into the cone, curving your file strokes to create soft, rounded indentations. Switch to a small barrette file to smooth the form.

9. Create a loop for the top of the cone out of sterling silver. Cut out a disk for the bottom of the cylinder from the sterling silver sheet. (The disk must be slightly larger than the circumference of the cylinder.) Solder each of these elements in place.

Constructing the Outer Cylinder

1. For the outer cylinder, measure and mark a rectangle on the sterling silver sheet. Here are two ways to calculate the length of the rectangle (the height remains the same): find a strip of wire that is the same thickness as the sterling sheet, and wrap it around the constructed cylinder; or measure the diameter of the constructed cylinder, add twice the thickness of the metal, and multiply by pi.

2. Saw out the sterling silver rectangle. File all edges clean and square. Bend the rectangle into a cylinder. Clean the joint, and solder closed. True up the cylinder as needed.

3. File and sand both cylinders as needed until one slides smoothly inside the other. If the outer cylinder is too large, remove a small strip of metal and resolder the joint. If the outer cylinder is too small, saw it open, insert a sterling silver strip, and resolder.

4. Holding a file at a consistent angle, file a uniform, lightly textured surface on the outer silver cylinder. Then file a pattern of notches randomly cut around the form. (Other filed patterns are possible, of course, or you could simply leave the cylinder plain.)

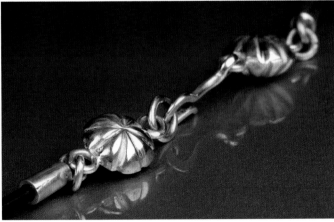

Creating the Clasp

1. To make a coordinated clasp for the necklace, saw out four 10 mm circles from the sterling silver sheet. Dap each circle to give it some contour. Sand the edges of the circles smooth. Solder each pair of domes together to make two small buttons. Mark, saw, and file grooves on the two small buttons that echo the grooves on the top of the cylinder.

2. To make the tubes that hold the leather cord, planish the sterling silver sheet to reduce its thickness. Mark a rectangle on the sterling silver sheet, and saw it out. Bend the rectangle into a tube. Solder the tube closed, and then cut it in half. Solder a small piece of sterling silver onto one end of each tube to make two end caps.

3. Make eight small sterling silver jump rings. Solder a partial jump ring to the top of each end cap. Solder two full jump rings to each button, directly across from each other. (To make a clean and strong joint, prepare the area by filing a curved recess in the edge of the button as needed.) Attach one side of one silver button to each end cap with a small jump ring.

4. Form a narrow strip of sterling silver sheet into a hook, and attach it to one silver button. Make a large jump ring to use as the catch, and attach it to the other silver button.

Finishing the Necklace

1. Clean up the locket and the clasp with small files and sandpaper. Polish the components either by hand with polishing papers or with a flexible shaft and buffs.

2. Secure the leather cord through the ring at the top of the locket. Measure 10 inches (25.4 cm) up the cord, and cut. Mix a small amount of epoxy, and press it into each end cap tube with a needle. Slide the leather into place, and let the epoxy cure.

3. Polish the metal one more time, and insert a lock of hair, shaving of unicorn horn, or whatever else you want into the locket.

Insight

Clearly the immediate appeal of the challenge was to incorporate widely diverse materials into a cohesive and interesting design. To do this while at the same time creating a project that was not so idiosyncratically quirky that someone else might want to make it required some reining in. In the end, I decided to take a minimalist approach and confine myself to a single material. I consider this a challenge of a different sort. The locket focuses on measurement to create cylinders that fit together so well that they don't clatter when worn but also don't require any force to lift them apart. It's a good feeling when you get that kind of precision right. The other skill I wanted to develop is the use of files and the rich world of opportunities that they can open. This project uses files to develop form, texture a surface, and create pattern.

artist: Tim McCreight

Design Number XXII

Created by **Todd Reed**

preserves stone's raw mystery…sits beautifully on the wearer…a brilliantly constructed box

Tools & Materials
Bench tool kit, page 6
Soldering kit, page 6
Soy sauce

Wildcard
Botryoidal hematite stone

From the Box

Method

Creating the Box

1. Measure and cut four 5.1 cm squares of the copper sheet. Two squares will be used for the bottom of the box and two for the lid.

2. Measure and cut a 20.3 x 5.1-cm strip from the copper sheet. This will be used for the sides of the box. Score and bend the strip into a square box. Solder the seam with silver solder.

3. Using your fingers, press in on the centers of the sides of the box to create the flower shape. Once you have made the shape that you want, solder it to one of the 5.1 cm copper squares.

4. For the top plate of the lid, fold one of the 5.1 cm copper squares in half, corner to corner. Forge the seam tight. Anneal the folded metal, and then open the seam. Forge the sheet flat.

5. Solder the folded and forged sheet to the top of the box. You now have a complete box form with six sides and a fold in the top.

6. Measure and scribe a line around the box that is 8 mm down from the top. Saw this line and cut off the top of the box.

7. Using a 1 mm bit, drill three holes in the lid of the box, all on one side of the fold. Cut three lengths of copper wire. Melt a ball on one end of each wire. From under the lid, thread the drilled holes with the balled silver wire.

8. Cut one of the 5.1-cm copper squares to fit inside the lid of the box. Solder this piece in place, leaving a 2 mm reveal. (The three silver wires are now trapped between the two plates that make the lid, and the lid fits nicely on the box.)

9. Cut a strip of silver sheet that is approximately 3 mm wide and long enough to go around all four sides of the lid. (This strip will hold the lid in the box.) Solder the strip on edge, approximately 1 mm inside the lid, shaping it as you go.

10. Determine how thick you want to make the shank of your ring. Cut a slit into the last 5.1 cm copper square that is slightly wider than the shank. (This slit will hold the shank of the ring when it is in the box.) Cut this piece of copper to fit inside the box. Level the copper inside the box, and solder it in place.

Making the Ring

1. Measure and cut a length of the sterling silver sheet to use for the bezel strip. Form the bezel strip to shape, and solder it to a piece of sterling silver sheet.

2. Measure and cut a strip of sterling silver to use for the ring shank. Form the strip into shape, and solder its ends under the bezel setting.

3. Set the stone into the bezel. Forge the edges of the band, and blacken the sterling silver. Complete the ring with a brush finish.

4. To patina the box and lid, clean them and then soak them overnight in soy sauce. The next day, slowly apply heat to patina the metal. Brush the surfaces with a coarse brush. Secure the pearls to the wires on top of the lid.

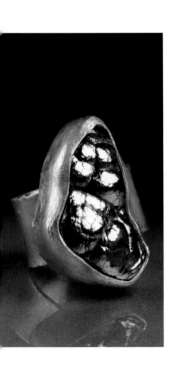

Insight

I don't get to do this type of work typically, so it seemed like a great opportunity to do something a bit different than I normally do. There was a pretty big selection of materials, so I didn't feel too restrained. Although there is an inherent challenge when looking at a box of materials that I do not typically use. My plan: come up with something that uses more and different types of raw.

I thought of some conventional ideas given the material and focused in on a hammered box idea. While looking through my stones one day, I thought I may never get a chance to use the hematite, so the box idea morphed a bit from there. The biggest challenge was to stay away from techniques and ideas I use in my everyday work and really try something different. The whole process was great although I didn't expect my busy travel schedule to get in the way as much as it did. This became a bit stressful, but that, too, is a part of any project: balance.

artist: Todd Reed

Created by **Janette Schuster**

Design Number XXIII

Design Number XXIII

tintypes provide story…

classic arch frames…

versatile orientation

Tools & Materials

Bench tool kit, page 6
Soldering kit, page 6
Photocopier
Rubber cement
Photocopied design template, page 125
Letter stamping set, ¹⁄₁₆ inch (1.6 mm)
Patina solution
Rub-on paste
Soft cloth
Draw plate or vise
Pin drill
Optional: rolling mill, gloss acrylic sealer, double-sided tape

Wildcard

Tintypes

From the Box

Method

Note: Unless otherwise specified, all holes are drilled with a 0.89 mm bit.

Cutting the Sheet Metals

1. To make a duplicate of the ½-inch (1.3 cm) washer, make a photocopy of the washer. Trim and use the photocopy as a template. Use metal shears to cut a 1-inch (2.5 cm) square from the copper sheet. Use rubber cement to attach the template to the copper square. Use a jeweler's saw to cut out the washer, piercing the interior with a drill to cut out the center of the washer. File and finish the washer with steel wool or sandpaper as needed, rounding the edges slightly to mimic the appearance of the washer.

2. If desired, use a rolling mill to thin the silver sheet to approximately 22 gauge. (This will make the pendant lighter to wear.) Use metal shears to cut a 5.7 x 6.4 cm piece of sterling silver sheet. Attach the design template to the cut silver sheet with rubber cement. Use a jeweler's saw to cut out the pendant base. File and finish the base with sandpaper or steel wool as needed. (I used steel wool to give the silver a brushed finish.) If desired, use a letter stamping set to stamp your initials on the center back of the silver base at this time.

Preparing the Tintypes & Washers

1. Choose tintypes of faces small enough to fit inside the ½-inch (1.3 cm) washers (Victorian "gem" tintypes are an ideal size).

Expert Tip: Tintypes can sometimes be thin, fragile, or peeling, and thus vulnerable to damage while working with them. To give added stability, consider temporarily backing them with a piece of scrap tintype or other thin metal sheet using rubber cement, or sealing them with gloss acrylic sealer.

---

2. Position the ½-inch (1.3 cm) washers over the tintypes to frame each face and form a "halo." Mark and use a saw to cut openings in the washers at the shoulders. (Tip: Make a copy of the tintypes and cut out the copy around the outline of the people. Use the copy as a template to cut out the washers.) File and finish the cut washer edges.

3. Using a letter stamping set, stamp names on the two ⁷⁄₁₆-inch (1.1 cm) washers. Stamp one name on each washer twice, once right-side up and once upside down, so each name can be read when the pendant is worn in either orientation. For consistent placement, draw a guideline circling the middle of the washer, and center your stamping on this guideline. Avoid positioning the letters in areas of the washer that will be cut out or riveted later. (Tip: Trace the washers on leftover copper sheet, and practice stamping to get the desired positioning and depth of imprint. A single hammer blow should suffice.)

4. Mark and use a saw to cut openings in the stamped washers. File and finish the cut edges. Mark and drill three holes in each of the four cut washers.

5. If desired, use a patina solution to give the washers a darkened, aged appearance. To make the stamped letters stand out more, apply black rub-on paste with a soft cloth, working it into the impressions, then wipe off the excess.

Making the Rivets & Assembling the Pendant

1. Cut the silver wire into 14 pieces, each 1 inch (2.5 cm) long. Cut 10 copper wire segments, each 1 inch (2.5 cm) long. Use a torch to melt a small ball on one end of each wire segment. Let each wire cool or drop it into water. Clean the balled wires with pickle or steel wool, or leave them dark for an aged appearance. Reserve two balled copper wires for later.

2. Trim any excess wire, seat each wire tightly in a draw plate or vise, and then shape the rivet head as desired. (I shape mine into a dome using a hammer and a concave watchmaker's tool. You can also shape each rivet head using a tiny file.)

"I chose Victorian tintypes as my wildcard, both for their relative durability (they don't need to be preserved behind glass or acrylic like paper photos) and unabashed romantic appeal."

3. Mark and drill holes at the four pointed corners of the silver base (refer to template for location). Set four purely decorative copper rivets in the holes.

4. Use double-sided tape or rubber cement to temporarily assemble the pendant elements. Mark the excess part of the tintypes for removal, disassemble the pendant elements, and trim the excess tintype with scissors or a saw, protecting the fragile images as much as possible. (At this point, if you have backed the tintypes with metal, remove the backing and rubber cement.)

5. Using the holes drilled in one of the ½-inch (1.3 cm) "halo" washers, drill matching holes in the tintype and silver base, and attach all three layers using silver rivets. (Tip: When riveting, drill all the holes in the top layer (washer), then drill the first matching hole in any middle layer (tintype) and bottom layer (silver base), and set the first rivet. Drill the second matching holes, set the rivet, and continue drilling and setting one rivet at a time.) Repeat this step for the second ½-inch (1.3 cm) "halo" washer, and then each stamped washer, attaching one washer at a time before moving on to the next.

6. In the silver base at the center of each stamped washer, mark and drill a hole for attaching the pearls later.

Preparing the Bails & Attaching the Pearls

1. Mark and use a saw to cut openings in two ⁵⁄₁₆-inch (8 mm) washers to be used as bails on the top and bottom of the pendant. File and finish the cut edges. Mark and drill two holes in

each washer. If desired, use patina solution to give the washers a darkened, aged appearance.

2. Drill matching holes in the silver base, and attach the bails using copper wire rivets.

3. Use a pin drill to ream two black pearls so they are fully drilled. Do this slowly and carefully by hand, dipping each pearl in water frequently to lubricate the drill bit and prevent the pearl from breaking.

4. A pearl is less likely to break when riveted if a washer is placed between it and the rivet head. To make tiny washers, use a hammer to planish the two copper balls (saved from step 1 of Making the Rivets & Assembling the Pendant) flat on a bench block. Drill a hole in the center of each ball. Cut the flattened balls off the wire and file them as needed to form washers. If desired, use a patina solution to give the washers a darkened appearance.

5. Use silver rivets to attach the tiny washers and pearls to the pendant. While riveting, use caution and gentle hammer blows, taking care not to overwork the rivets or break the pearls.

Preparing & Attaching Cord

1. Measure and cut the leather cord in the desired necklace length plus 1½ inches (3.8 cm). (This project features a 24-inch [61 cm] cord.)

2. To make an end cap at one end of the cord, fold over approximately ¾ inch (1.9 cm) of cord. About 3 mm from the end, drill a hole through the center of both layers of the cord. Cut about 6 inches (15.2 cm) of copper wire, thread about ¾ inch (1.9 cm) of the wire through both holes in the cord, and bend the short end of the wire up, parallel to the folded end of the cord. Holding the folded end of the cord and short end of the wire together tightly with pliers, wrap the long end of the wire around the cord about eight times to form a coiled end cap, moving the pliers along and out of the way as you continue to coil. Trim both ends of the wire, and tuck them in using pliers. Be sure to leave about a 6 mm loop of cord at the end of the coil. Trim the tip of the cord as needed, and use a marker to blacken the light center of the cord, if desired. Repeat this step for the other end of the cord.

3. To make a toggle closure, use one ⁵⁄₁₆-inch (8 mm) washer as the loop. Use a saw to cut a 7.9 x 3 mm bar from the copper sheet. Round the edges of the bar with a file. Drill a center hole using a 1.32 mm bit and a hole at each end using a 0.89 mm bit.

4. For wire wrapping the closure, cut two lengths of copper wire, each approximately 4 inches (10.2 cm). If desired, use a patina solution to give the wire, washer, bar, and coiled ends of the cord a darkened, aged appearance. Use wire wrapping to attach the washer and bar to the loops at the ends of the leather cord.

5. Fold the cord in half to form a loop, thread the loop through the pendant bail from front to back, and pull several inches of the loop through. Thread the ends of the cord through the loop, and pull them tightly to form a knot at the bail. To wear the pendant upside down, loosen the knot at the bail, pull the ends of the cord back out of the loop, and remove the cord. Flip the pendant upside down, and repeat this process to reattach the cord.

Insight

Although the initial design for the necklace came to me fairly intuitively, I still found the experience challenging in a number of ways, which is one reason I agreed to participate in the first place. Being a found-object artist, rarely do I work from a design sketch or use all "new" raw materials. While we were allowed to use additional jewelry findings like rivets and closures in our pieces, I set myself the added challenge of using just what was inside the box to make any findings I needed. By limiting my materials even further, I was forced to enter unfamiliar territory. This included practicing some traditional jewelry techniques still new to me (such as using a rolling mill and firing up a torch to make rivets) and getting acquainted with materials I don't often use (like sterling sheet and leather cord). But in this jewelry making experience as in all else, with challenge came the potential to learn and grow, for which I'm grateful.

The found-object artist in me was immediately drawn to the copper washers with their intended life as industrial hardware rather than jewelry components, so I made them an important element in my design. I also added some familiar "friends" in the form of old photos. These captured moments in time are just about my favorite art material, so I chose Victorian tintypes as my wildcard, both for their relative durability (they don't need to be preserved behind glass or acrylic like paper photos) and unabashed romantic appeal.

artist: Janette Schuster

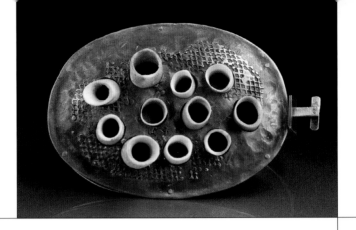

Design Number XXIV

Created by **Eric Silva**

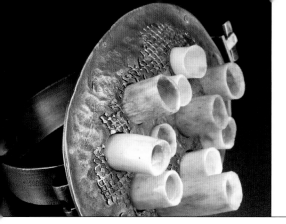

best of two distinct design styles...
modern hinge and fused setting...
primitive yet elegant wildcard

Materials & Tools
Bench tool kit, page 6
Soldering kit, page 6
Disk cutter
Mandrel
3 mm square sterling silver wire

Wildcard
Antler

Process

Creating the Top of the Bracelet

1. Use a permanent marker to draw the desired shape, such as a large oval, on the copper sheet. Use the jeweler's saw to cut out the metal. File the cut edges.

2. Form the copper shape into a shallow bowl using the forming hammer and the wood block.

3. Draw a series of circles inside the copper form. Drill a hole in each circle, and saw out the shapes. File the cut edges of the interior circles.

4. Flow solder on the top surface of the copper form, and connect the wire mesh.

5. Place the copper form on top of the sterling silver sheet, and trace its outline. Saw out the sterling silver shape, and file the cut edges. (This is the bottom layer of the bracelet.)

6. Cut and carve the antler with a flexible shaft to fit in the holes in the copper top. Make sure to carve the antler so each piece is larger at one end than at the other. This way, they won't fall through the holes.

7. With the bowl of the copper facing up, fit the antler pieces in the holes. Place the

"The real challenge was to contain all the materials in one piece that resonated my ideas."

From the Box

sterling silver piece on top of the copper. Turn the assembly over, taking care not to loosen the antler pieces.

8. On each side of the assembly, drill three small, evenly spaced holes through both the copper and sterling silver layers. Cut six short lengths of the copper wire to use as rivets. Rivet the copper and sterling silver layers together.

Creating the Ball Hinge

1. Use a disk cutter to cut two sterling silver disks, each 6 mm in diameter. Dome each disk in a dapping block. Solder the domes together to make a small ball.

2. Select two copper washers, and dome each in the dapping block. Solder the two domed copper washers over the small sterling silver ball.

Forming the Bracelet Band

1. Cut two 5.1 cm strips of sterling silver sheet. Solder the ball hinge to one end of one sterling silver strip. Bend the opposite end of this strip around a mandrel that is approxi-

mately 8 mm in diameter. Once the end meets the rest of the strip, bend the strip back in the opposite direction. Make a gentle arc in the metal between this bend and the ball hinge.

2. On the other strip, measure and mark a centered 4 mm square that is approximately 4 mm from one end. Drill a small hole inside the square, and saw out the interior shape. This is the slide catch for the bracelet.

3. Cut two small strips of sterling silver, each 1.7 x 0.4 cm. File the cut edges, and round the corners. Saw one small, angled slit near one corner of each strip. Make the slit wide enough to accommodate 18-gauge sheet. On the opposite end of each small strip, drill a small centered hole approximately 3 mm from the end.

4. Slide the slit of one small strip onto one corner of the long, straight strip at the end without the pierced square. Solder the strips together. Repeat with the second small strip on the opposite corner of the same end.

5. Drill a hole straight through the ball inside the joint. Position the drilled short

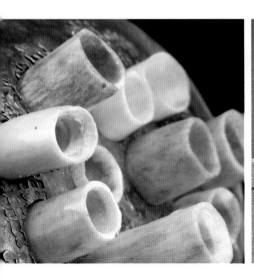

strips on either side of the ball. Feed a piece of tubing through the strips and the ball. Cut the tubing, leaving enough length to make a rivet. Rivet the small strips to the ball.

Making the Clasp

1. Saw out a small, 1 x 0.3 cm strip of sterling silver sheet. File the cut edges, and round the corners. Saw out a 1.1 cm length of 3 mm square sterling silver wire. Mark a point that is 7 mm in from one end of the square wire. Saw a centered slit in the square wire, ending at the marked point.

2. Insert the small silver strip into the wire's slit. Center the strip in the slit. Drill a hole that passes through all three layers of metal. Cut a piece of copper rivet wire, and rivet these elements together. (The small strip should turn freely inside the slit.) Solder the opposite end of the square wire under the bracelet.

3. Make a gentle arc in the metal so that the square hole stretches to fit over the square wire. Turn the small strip to secure the bracelet.

Insight

My first thought was that this was going to be fun, but the materials seemed like a lot for one piece. Then, knowing that I didn't need to use it all, I started focusing on the components that would work for me. I liked the idea that there were mechanical elements to add to the work like washers. I didn't put too much thought into the planning. Instead, I used my skill set and figured out how it would work as I went along. The real challenge was to contain all the materials in one piece that resonated my ideas. I chose antler as my wildcard since it's familiar in my own work, and I knew how it would react to the other materials in the box. I enjoyed the challenge. It was freeing in a way. I haven't had a chance to work on one thing for three days in a while.

artist: Eric Silva

Created by **Tod Pardon**

Design Number XXV

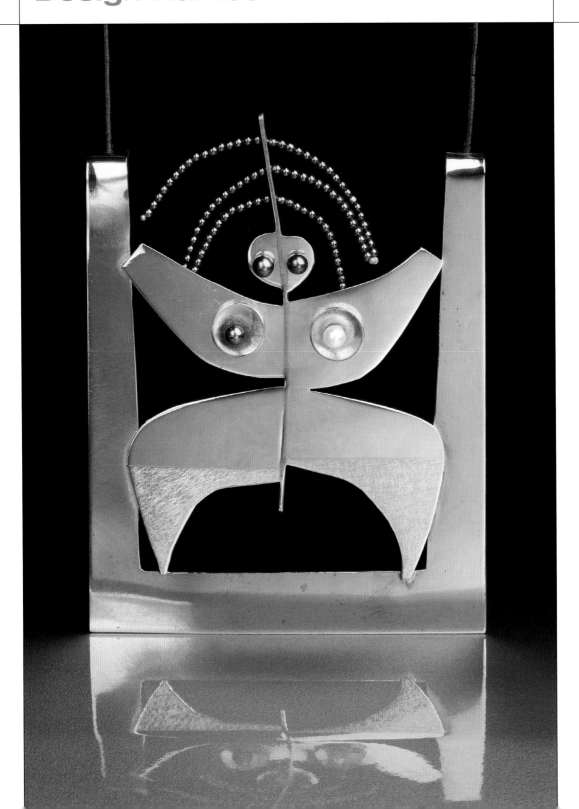

looks forward and back...

figure gives life to piece...

subtle contrast of finishes

Materials & Tools
Bench tool kit, page 6
Soldering kit, page 6
Drill press (optional)
Quick-drying epoxy
Draw plate

Wildcard
Hematite beads, 2 mm,
 1 to 2 strands

From the Box

Method

Creating the Figure

1. Scribe a 10.2 cm x 6 mm strip on the copper sheet. Cut out the strip with a jeweler's saw. From one end of the strip, measure and mark three centered points that are 3 mm apart. Punch the metal at the marked points, and drill holes with a 1.02 mm bit.

2. Mark four 3.8 cm squares on the sterling silver sheet. Draw shapes for the figure's arms/torso and legs in the marked quadrants. (Refer to the project photo for possibilities.) With a pencil or felt marker, mark the shapes 1T and 2T for the top (torso) and 1B and 2B for the bottom (legs). Saw out the four drawn and labeled shapes.

3. Using the leftover silver sheet, saw a freehand circle that is approximately 1.6 cm in diameter. Cut the circle in half to make the figure's head.

4. Position the copper strip on edge on a flat soldering pad. Arrange the sterling silver figure on either side of the copper strip. Solder the pieces together with medium solder, and pickle the piece. File or use belt sander to flatten and smooth the surface.

Creating & Connecting the Copper Swing

1. Place the metal figure on top of a 4-inch (10.2 cm) copper square. Adjust the position of the figure so it sits low on the square. Draw the exterior points of the figure on the copper, and then scribe lines that are just inside the marked lines. (This gives

"It was like a wonderful game: this beautiful aluminum box came in the mail with the playing pieces nicely wrapped. Or maybe like a puzzle where you have control of the pieces, and it's your job to work to fit them together on a yet-to-be-determined board. "

you enough room to solder the figure to the copper later.) Using the scribed lines as a guide, saw out an irregular U or swing-shape piece of the copper. File the edges smooth.

2. Place the silver figure facedown and flat on the soldering pad. Place the copper U shape on top of it so a small part of the arms and legs of the piece are touching the copper. The silver "head" should not extend above the copper U shape. Solder the forms together with medium silver solder, and pickle the piece.

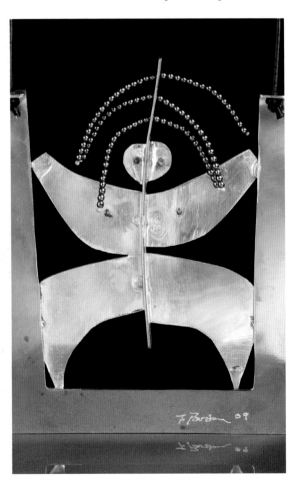

3. On each end of the copper U, measure down 3 mm and mark a centered point. Punch and drill each mark with a 2.38 mm bit. On each end of the copper U, measure down 6 mm and mark a line across the copper. With parallel pliers, bend the copper at the marked line to a 90° angle. Round off edges of the U with a file.

4. Punch two circles out of the leftover copper, each 1.3 cm in diameter. Dome each circle in a dapping block. Punch and drill a hole in the center of both domes with a 1.02 mm bit. File the burrs off the backs of the domes.

5. Polish the pendant and the domes on a polishing machine to a high shine. Clean the metal.

Adding the Details & Hair

1. Position a dome on both sides of the figure's torso, with the concave surface of the dome pointing up. Mark the center of the disks on the silver torso. Punch and drill a hole at each marked point with a 1.02 mm bit.

2. To make the figure's eyes, mark, punch, and drill a hole with a 1.02 mm bit on both sides of the figure's head (the freehand circle element).

3. Cut four pieces of sterling silver wire, each ½ inch (1.3 cm) long. Melt one end of each wire into a small ball.

4. Mix a small amount of quick-drying epoxy. Feed one balled wire through the back of one eyehole. Cut the wire so the black pearl will fit snugly to the surface of the piece. Glue the pearl on the wire with a small amount of epoxy. Use the same method to adhere the second eye.

5. Feed a balled wire through the back of each hole in the torso. Slide a copper dome onto each wire with the concave surfaces facing up. Cut the wires so one black pearl fits snugly against the dome on one side and one white pearl fits snugly on the other. Adhere the pearls to the wires with epoxy.

6. Draw the remaining silver wire through a draw plate, thinning it to 24 gauge. Cut a 4-inch (10.2 cm) length of the wire, and melt one end into a ball. Find and mark the center of the wire, taking into consideration that you will be balling the other end. String the 2 mm hematite beads onto the wire until you reach the marked center point. Feed the wire through the lowest hole in the copper strip. String hematite beads on the rest of the wire, leaving enough room to ball the end. Make sure the beads are tight on the wire and then ball the end, taking care not to overheat the nearest bead. Repeat this process with the remaining two pieces of wire. Adjust the wire lengths if desired to create a different hairstyle.

Completing the Necklace

1. Using a straightedge, scribe a line across the bottom of the legs. Under this line, use a scribe to draw a pattern of small circles, scratching the surface of the silver.

2. Polish the piece with a buffing wheel, and clean it. Thread one end of the leather cord through a hole at the top of the copper "swing." Tie a small tight knot in the cord. Determine where you want the pendant to hang (remembering that it's going to slip over your head). Tie off the other end of the cord, and cut off any excess.

Insight

It's been a long-standing practice of mine not to do commissions. But when I received this proposal I found it hard to resist the challenge. It was like a wonderful game: this beautiful aluminum box came in the mail with the playing pieces nicely wrapped. Or maybe like a puzzle where you have control of the pieces, and it's your job to work to fit them together on a yet-to-be-determined board.

This project took me into areas I hadn't been before and that's where you learn new things. Even though it's in the same direction, it makes you take a different path than normal. Since I only make one-of-a-kind pieces, it was a challenge to make something that was reproducible by directions.

artist: Tod Pardon

Design Number XXVI

Created by **Kristin Lora**

alchemy of bimetal...motion, sound, and shimmer...organic yet refined...finishes create perfect contrast

Tools & Materials

Bench tool kit, page 6
Soldering kit, page 6
Abrasive wheel attachment
Disk cutter
Patina
Rotary tumbler
Awl

Wildcard

Bimetal, 18-karat gold, 22 gauge

From the Box

Method

1. Cut two 1.6 x 3.8 cm strips of 18-gauge sterling silver sheet. Using a rolling mill, thin the strips to approximately 22 gauge. Cleanly cut two 1.6 x 3.5 cm strips from the thinned silver sheets.

2. Use a triangle file to create a random pattern on one end of both silver strips. With round-nose pliers, bend each metal strip into an oval shape—first bend the unmarked end of the strip, and then the patterned end, overlapping the ends. Solder the overlapped silver strips, and sand the top and bottom edges of each. These ovals are the base shape of the earrings.

3. On the narrow sides of each oval, mark two centered points directly across from each other and approximately 3 mm down from the top edge. Drill 1.6 mm holes at each point to hold the tube rivet. Drill random tiny holes on all sides of each oval. Use a round file inside the ovals to clean off all burrs.

4. Solder a small piece of the leftover silver strip onto an open end of each oval form, capping the top of the earrings. Pickle the oval forms, and clean their edges. Polish all sides with an abrasive wheel attachment on the flexible shaft.

5. Make two small jump rings from the 20-gauge sterling silver wire. Center and solder one jump ring to the top of each earring.

6. To make the dangles, cut the 18-gauge sterling silver sheet into 10 very thin strips, each

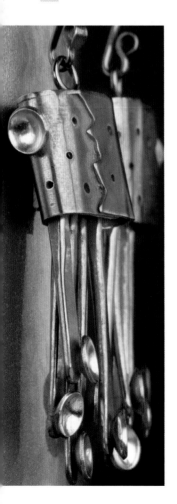

approximately 1 mm wide. Cut the thin strips at random lengths, ranging from 2.5 to 3.6 cm. (Different lengths will give the strips variety when they hang.)

7. Hammer the thin strips to give them texture. Hammer one end of all the strips flat and wide, and then change directions to hammer the other end of all the strips, stretching them in a perpendicular direction. Polish, clean, and smooth all sides of the strips with a kitchen scrub pad. Drill a 1.8 mm centered hole near one end of each flattened strip.

8. Using the disk cutter, cut 12 small circles from the bimetal sheet, each 5 mm in diameter. Dap the circles so they are slightly domed, with the gold surface on the concave side.

9. Cut two pieces of the sterling silver tubing, each slightly longer than the width of the earrings. This extra length provides the material for your rivets.

10. With the gold side facing out, solder one bimetal dome onto each non-drilled end of the hammered silver strips. Also solder one dome, gold side out, on one end of each piece of tubing. Pickle the components, and clean up any rough edges.

11. Form a pair of simple ear wires out of the 20-gauge sterling silver wire. Darken all of the components in a blackening solution, such as liver of sulfur. Tumble the blackened components in a rotary tumbler with steel shot.

12. For each earring, determine the order in which you want to assemble the five dangling strips. Feed the tube through the rivet hole in one end of the oval. Place the five dangling strips on the tube. Thread the tube through the opposite rivet hole. Use an awl to expand the tube end, securing the rivet. Place one ear wire on top of each earring.

Insight

I'm always inspired by projects with some kind of constraints—themes, materials, etc.—as it pushes me to create things I might not otherwise make. When I received the box of supplies, I felt somewhat limited. I wasn't feeling inspired by the copper so I needed to come up with my ideas using the silver items—and there weren't a lot. I opened the box and let them just sit for several days, occasionally observing them, before I had some thoughts on what to make. This challenge made me realize how easy it is to rely on the variety of ready-made or fabricated materials available. For example, the sheet of silver was a really thick gauge, and it's so easy to just buy the gauge I need rather than modify.

artist: Kristin Lora

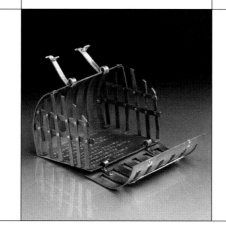

Design Number XXVII

Created by **Chihiro Makio**

Design Number XXVII

an engineering marvel...
maximizes supplies and
function of piece...multiple
configurations

Materials & Tools

Bench tool kit, page 6
Soldering kit, page 6
Photocopied template, page 127
  (donut shape for end of copper tube)
Liver of sulfur solution
Magnet clasps, 6 sets
Bag of sterling silver posts,
  100 with "head"
Tie pin and backing
Alphabet stamping tools (optional)

Wildcard

2 glass tubes, 1.9 cm outside
  diameter, each 2.9 cm long

From the Box

Method

Constructing the Copper Containers

1. Cut a strip 1½ inches (3.8 cm) wide from the copper sheet. Using a rolling mill, thin the copper strip to 22 gauge. Measure the diameter of the glass tube. Use this measurement to make a matching copper tube. (I wrapped the strip around a dapping punch.) Solder the seam of the copper tube, and file its ends. Repeat this process to make a total of three copper tubes. (These will be referenced as the copper "containers.")

2. Cut a 5.1 cm strip off the 18-gauge copper sheet. Use a rolling mill to thin the strip to 24 gauge. Transfer the photocopied template onto the copper sheet six times. Saw and pierce out these shapes for the ends of the containers. (Save the copper circles cut out from the interior of the forms. You'll use them later when making the earrings.)

3. Solder a pierced copper shape on each end of all the containers, and clean off excess. Slice each container in half lengthwise along the soldered line. Use a round file to make a groove on adjacent sides of each sliced container. (The groove will seat the sterling silver tubing that will be used for the hinge.)

4. Cut 15 lengths of sterling silver tubing, each 6 mm long. Solder three small silver tubes on one grooved edge and two silver tubes on the opposite edge. Work-harden a length of copper or silver wire, insert a piece into each hinge, and rivet the ends.

5. Create a tube out of the 22-gauge copper sheet that is 10 mm in diameter. Slice this tube into 5 mm sec-

tions. Solder one tube onto each end of the copper containers, making sure the tubes are straight and aligned so the container closes tightly. (Save the remaining tube sections for later.)

6. Use a rolling mill to thin the silver sheet to 26 gauge. Cut three 5 x 25 mm strips to make the clasps for each container. Solder one end of a silver strip to the inner wall of one side of a copper container. On the other side of the container, drill a small hole near the inner edge. Solder a tiny piece of copper wire in the drilled hole. Drill a hole in the silver clasp where the wire will rest, and make sure it catches. Solder a small piece of silver tubing on the end of the clasp to use as a latch. Repeat this process to attach a clasp to each container.

7. Roll six large copper washers through the rolling mill until they are thinner and slightly warped. Dap the washers, bending them to the same curve as the container walls. Trace an inner circle on the washers, and pierce out. Determine which washers will go on which containers. Holding them in place, drill four to five holes through each washer and through the container.

8. Clean and color all metal components as desired. (On this project, I used heat patinas sealed with lacquer, liver of sulfur solutions with a brass-brushed finish, as well as fully polished surfaces.)

9. Cut six silver mesh ovals to match the outer diameter of the copper washers. Curve the mesh ovals to match the curve of the washers. Sandwich the mesh ovals between the washers and the container. Push a sterling silver earring post from the outside to the inside of the container, passing through the holes in the copper washers and the mesh. Snip extra wire off the post, and rivet from the inside to secure.

Making the Glass Tubes with the End Caps

1. Cut the silver sheet in half. Use the rolling mill to thin one piece of the silver to 24 gauge. Anneal the thinned sheet, and hammer it flat.

2. Make four 24-gauge silver bands, each 3 mm wide, to wrap around the ends of the glass tubes. Cut four 24-gauge silver circles that are the same diameter as the bands. On each silver circle, pierce and cut out an interior circle, leaving small triangles at 6 and 12 o'clock. (Reserve the interior cutouts for use when making the ring.) Solder one band to each circle. Clean, buff, and oxidize.

3. Roll four medium washers through the rolling mill until each is slightly larger than the band made in step 2. Clean the interior hole of each washer. Feed a copper tube (created in step 5, Constructing the Copper Containers) inside each washer, and solder together.

4. Cut a strip of 24-gauge silver that is 3 mm wide and longer than the diameter of the washer's interior circle. Bend the strips to make flaps that will just overlap the ends of the triangles on the silver bands. File the ends of the flaps at an angle, so that when you turn the washer on the end band it will close tightly. File the edge of the tube flat, solder the strip with the flaps across the tube, and cut off the excess strip inside the tube. File ridges on the outside of the washers so you can get a nice grip on them. Clean the metal, and apply a heat patina. (To further embellish this piece, I drilled the washer's surface and hammered molten silver scraps into the holes.)

5. Measure the length of the capped glass tubes and the length of the copper containers. These elements should be the same length. If not, file the ends of the tubes on the copper containers.

Making the Ring & Brooch "Settings"

1. Cut three 3 mm wide strips of 18-gauge sterling silver sheet. Mark two of the strips with four points, each signifying a 90° scored and bent angle. Score the metal at these points, bend the angles in the strip, and then fill each bend with solder. With the third strip, bend and solder a band for the ring. Cut four small rectangles out of scrap silver sheet. Solder the rectangles at the points.

2. File and clean the edges of the silver left over from step 2 of Making the Glass Tubes with the End Caps. Dome the circles with a dapping punch.

3. Assemble the band, one scored, bent, and reinforced strip, and two domed disks for the ring setting. Solder these elements together. There should be just enough tension between the domes to securely hold the glass tubes or the copper containers.

4. To make the brooch setting, cut two small squares out of the 18-gauge silver. These will be the pin catch and joint. Drill the center point of both squares. Cut one square into the shape. Assemble one bent strip, two domed disks, and the pin catch and joint, and solder these elements together. Feed one end of a silver wire through the hole in the pin joint, and melt it into a ball. Wrap the remaining wire around the joint a few times, and then feed under the catch. Trim and file the wire to a sharp point.

Creating the Flowers

1. Cut six small rings out of the 26-gauge silver sheet, making one slightly larger than the others.

Dome the rings in a dapping block. Solder a backing sheet onto each ring, and drill a hole at the center point.

2. Cut out 30 teardrop shapes in assorted sizes from the leftover 26-gauge silver and copper sheet. Arrange six petals in a flower shape, and solder together at the center. Repeat to make a total of five flowers. Drill a hole in the center of each flower.

3. Pair each flower with a domed ring. (You will have one domed ring left over to use later.) Feed a length of wire (copper or silver) through the center holes of each pair. Leave a little wire sticking out of the front of each ring for a pearl post. Leave approximately 4 cm of wire sticking out the back of each flower. Solder together the flower, the ring, and the wire. Clean the metal, and finish it as desired. Gently curve the flower petals forward. Glue a pearl onto each wire post. Curl the wire on the back of the flower into a spiral. Hammer the wire to workharden it so that the spiral will work as a clasp.

Creating the Butterflies

1. Cut six small wing shapes from leftover sterling silver sheet. For each butterfly, cut three small pieces of tubing. Center and solder one tube on the interior edge of one wing shape. Position and solder two tubes on the adjacent wing shape, leaving a gap for the tube from the other wing shape.

2. Cut two silver wires, and solder them into a Y shape. At the top of the Y, ball one end and coil the other. Feed the bottom of the Y-shaped wire

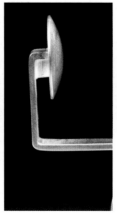

> **"When I saw the silver mesh, I knew that I was going to make something that could be looked through, which is where my wildcard came in."**

through the tube hinge, connecting the wing shapes into a butterfly. Coil the end of the wire.

3. Bend several pieces of copper and silver wire into S shapes. Hammer the wires to work-harden them.

Making the Leather Flowers

1. Cut three long pieces of leather cord to make the large flower. Cut three short pieces of leather cord to make the small flower. Cut a small strip of copper for each length of leather cord. Curl the narrow ends of each strip up. Feed each cord through a curled strip, and then pinch the curls on each strip to secure the cords. Drill a hole through the center point of each copper strip.

2. Roll a copper washer through the rolling mill, and dome it in a dapping block. Cut a true circle in the center of the domed washer, and file all edges. Make a 26-gauge silver bezel to fit around the domed washer. Drill a hole through the center of the back sheet of the bezel.

3. Cut and dome a copper disk that matches the diameter of the bezel. Solder a wire to the center of the concave side of the disk. Feed the other end of the wire through the three large petal layers and through the hole in the back of the bezel. Rivet to secure.

4. Cut and dome a piece of silver screen to fit inside the washer. Rivet the washer, and dome together with silver wire rivets. Set the mesh-filled washer in the silver bezel. Solder a pin tack on the convex side of the copper dome.

5. Cut and dome a copper disk to match the remaining silver domed ring (from step 3 of Creating the Flowers). Solder a copper wire onto the convex side of the dome. Feed the wire through the three small petal groupings and through the silver domed ring. Glue a half-drilled pearl to the end of the wire to secure.

Creating the Magnet Clasps

1. Cut six silver and 17 copper 1.3 cm circles out of the leftover sheet metal. Slightly dome five of the copper circles, and drill each in the center. Dome six silver and six copper circles deeper to make semi-spheres. Drill two holes near the top of each semi-sphere that are 3 mm apart. Cut 2 cm lengths of silver wire, and melt one end of each into a ball.

2. Insert a wire into a semi-sphere, feed it through a magnetic clasp, guide it out of the semi-sphere, and thread it through a shallow disk. Take care to fill all silver semi-spheres with positive magnets and all copper semi-spheres with negative magnets. Ball the second end of the wire. Drill two holes in the copper dome on the back of the smaller leather flower. Follow this assembly process to connect a silver semi-sphere magnet to one hole and one copper semi-sphere magnet to the other.

Constructing the Basket

1. Use the rolling mill to thin the last 6.4 cm strip of 18-gauge copper so you'll have enough sheet to make the basket. Transfer the photocopied template onto the copper sheet. Score the folding line, and pierce out the 12 openings. Reserve the cutout material to use as the vertical pieces on the sides of the basket.

2. Arrange two sets of six strips in a fence-like pattern. On each set, position the outside strips and one inside strip lower than the rest so they can later be riveted to the bottom of the basket. Cut four additional 3 mm strips of copper to use as the horizontal pieces on the sides of the basket. Rivet the "fences" together with sterling silver earring posts.

3. Dome the pierced section of the sheet, and then cut the dome in half so the curves on both sides of the basket match. Rivet the side pieces to the basket, and trim their tops to echo the curve of the basket.

4. On the copper sheet for the bottom of the basket, pierce and saw out two small rectangles. Each rectangle should be on one long edge of the sheet, 1 cm inside the corner and 3 mm from the edge. Optional: Stamp the list of materials used on the copper sheet that will become the bottom of the basket. Make a plaque with the title of the piece to attach to the basket later. Bend the back of the basket on the scored line.

5. Cut two 2.9 cm copper strips, and rivet one end of each strip to the "door" of the basket. Feed the opposite ends of the strips through the pierced rectangles on the bottom of the basket, and curl them up. These are the "hinges" for the door.

6. Cut two silver strips, each approximately 3 mm wide x 3.5 cm long. Cut two 3 x 6 mm silver strips. Solder one of these short strips to each of the longer silver strips, approximately 6 mm from one end.

7. On the top of the back half of the basket, pierce and saw out two small rectangles. Each rectangle should be approximately 3 mm inside the edge and 1.5 cm from one corner. Feed the straight end of one silver strip into each rectangle, and curl them up. These are the hinges for the basket's latches.

8. Oxidize the whole basket, and then sand the stamped sheet inside to highlight the letters. Oxidize the letters on the plaque, brass brush the whole piece, and rivet the plaque to the front of the basket.

9. Slightly dome two of the leftover copper circles. Solder a sterling silver earring post to the center of each dome on the convex side. This is the basic earring device that you mix and match with many of the decorative elements.

Insight

While planning my project, I was a little torn between making a design that would be recognizable as mine—my signature technique is hand-stitched details on the edge of metal—or having fun and trying something totally different. I decided on the latter. When I saw the silver mesh, I knew that I was going to make something that could be looked through, which is where my wildcard came in. I picked Pyrex tubes; I like that the tubes don't take away from the other nine materials but have a very different quality—in this case, the transparency. In addition to using up the provided materials and making as many items as possible, my other immediate thought was to make sections that would be interchangeable so the wearer has many options. I love jewelry that the wearer can play with.

artist: Chihiro Makio

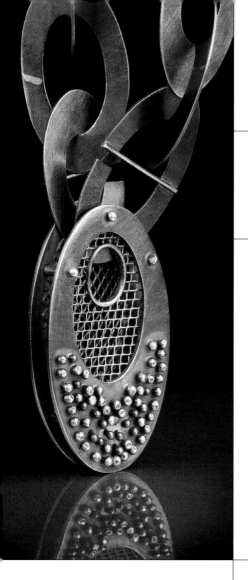

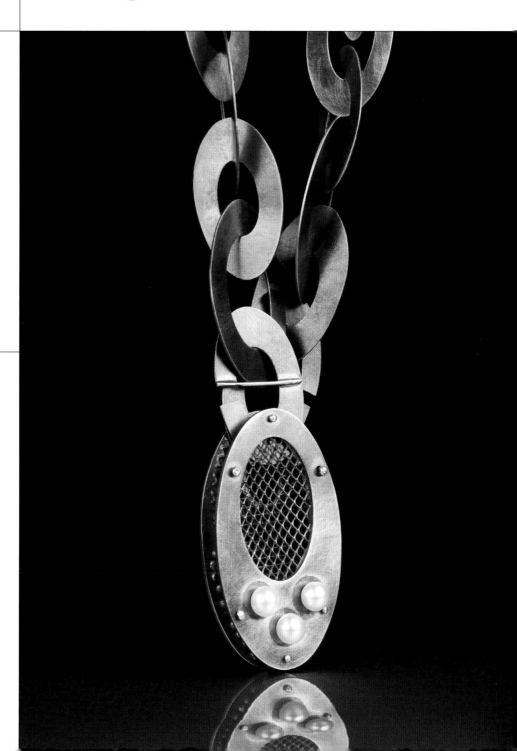

inventive clasp makes
uncommon connection…
versatile central pendant…
romantic with a clean edge

Tools & Materials

Bench tool kit, page 6
Soldering kit, page 6
Photocopied design template,
   page 126
Liver of sulfur
Two-part epoxy

Wildcard

None

Method

Creating the Chain & Clasp

1. Create six to eight additional large washers by tracing their outlines on the copper and silver sheets. (You will need at least 25 washers. I used 16 copper and nine silver ones.) Make sure to conserve as much of the sterling silver sheet as possible, as you will need it for the pendant. Pierce and saw out the new washers. File all cut edges, both inside and out, and sand to a 400-grit finish.

2. Set the rollers of the rolling mill slightly closer than the thickness of the washers. Roll one washer through at a time, and then close the rollers more. Roll each washer through again, making sure to place the tip of the elongated washer in the rolling mill first. This method elongates the washers, making them oval. Repeat this method until the ovals range from 2.5 to 4.4 cm long. Do not make the ovals too thin or they won't have enough integrity to act as necklace links.

3. Lay out the ovals in a line and arrange them as you like for the chain. (I grouped five silver ovals together in one section and four silver ovals in another section.) Saw open every other oval in the middle of its length. Link the whole ovals into the sawed ovals to make a chain, closing the sawed ovals as you would close a jump ring.

4. Make sure that each sawed oval has a flush and close joint, and then solder the ovals closed with hard solder. File and sand the soldered ovals to a 400-grit finish.

5. At the two ends of the chain, center a length of sterling silver wire across the back of the last ovals. Solder the wires in place. On one side of the ovals, use a jeweler's saw to cut an opening 4 mm wide above the soldered wire. Sand the openings smooth.

From the Box

"I've found that my customers like versatile jewelry, so I thought I'd make a reversible pendant and also make it removable, so one could just wear the chain without any further decoration."

Making the Pendant

1. Using the photocopied template, trace the ovals—A & B— onto the sterling silver sheet, and saw them out. Pierce and saw out the inner oval from both forms. File and sand all cut edges.

2. On both ovals, use a scribe or punch to mark the locations for the wire rivet holes. On oval A, use a scribe or punch to mark three locations at which you will drill and saw out three circles for the copper domes that hold the pearls. On oval B, use a scribe or punch to mark where you want to drill holes for the decorative balled wires. Drill all marked holes with a 0.75 mm bit.

3. Use a marker to draw two ovals onto the silver mesh, each slightly larger than the interior ovals on A & B. Cut out the mesh ovals with snips or scissors.

4. Solder one mesh piece onto each silver oval with easy solder, taking care not to melt the mesh. Make sure to aim the heat of the torch mainly at the silver sheet, not the mesh.

Expert Tip: You can use powder solder to make sure each square of the screen is securely soldered or solder snippets for this operation.

---

5. Follow the template to make an oval out of the sterling silver wire. Solder the joint of the wire oval with easy solder. Solder the wire oval onto the mesh on oval B, taking care not to melt the mesh. Use snips to cut out the mesh inside the wire oval. Sand the interior of the small oval.

6. To make the balls on oval B, cut 1 cm lengths of copper wire and silver wire. Ball up one end of each wire with a torch. Thread each wire through a hole in oval B, then ball the other end. Make sure to leave the holes for the rivets empty. (If you forget, you can simply cut out those wires later.) In this project, the copper wires are grouped in the center of the arrangement.

7. On oval A, use a jeweler's saw to cut out the holes for the copper domes and pearls. (Refer to the template as needed.) Sand the holes perfectly round.

8. Mark three 8 mm circles on the copper sheet, and cut them out with a jeweler's saw. Dome the copper circles with a dap and a dapping block so they fit into the holes in oval A. With the concave sides of the domes

facing forward, solder the domes to oval A with easy solder. File and sand the domes flush with the oval.

9. To make the pegs for the pearls, snip three 5 mm lengths of copper wire and file all ends flat. Using easy solder, solder one wire to the center of each concave dome. Sand oval A and oval B to a 400-grit finish.

10. Cut six 5 mm lengths of sterling silver tubing. File and sand the cut ends. Cut six 1 cm lengths of sterling silver wire. Ball one end of each wire piece. Thread a silver wire through a rivet hole in oval B, then through a length of tubing, then through the corresponding hole in oval A. Double-check that the sides of the ovals are facing the correct way. Ball the wire to secure the two sides of the pendant. Repeat this process for the remaining rivet holes.

Finishing the Necklace

1. Rub the pendant and each link of the chain with a green kitchen scrub for a matte finish. Blacken each component in a liver of sulfur solution. Rub the blackened elements with fine-grit steel wool so small areas of copper and silver will subtly shine through the patina.

2. Mix together a small amount of two-part epoxy, glue the white pearls onto their pegs, and let dry.

3. Attach the chain to any two rivet spacers on the pendant. Alter where you attach the chain to create a different look.

Insight

I felt that the challenge was too easy! I wish we had fewer materials to work with that actually made it hard to come up with different projects. There were so many materials that the challenge came from deciding what to make instead of deciding how to use the materials. I designed my necklace based on skills that I thought would be interesting like making ovals from round washers using a rolling mill. It's an "aha" moment for some people, so that's how I made the chain. I've found that my customers like versatile jewelry, so I thought I'd make a reversible pendant and also make it removable, so one could just wear the chain without any further decoration.

artist: Joanna Gollberg

Design Number XXIX

Created by **Sarah Hood**

drama in size and scale...

brilliant prong setting...

flawlessly incorporates
stand

Tools & Materials

Bench tool kit, page 6
Soldering kit, page 6
Ring mandrel
Sanding wheel, cutoff disks, or
    whatever is desired for texture
Cup burrs
Liver of sulfur
Clear lacquer (optional)
Bezel pusher

Wildcard

Prehnite, 12 mm round faceted

From the Box

Method

Creating the Band

1. Scribe a line in the sterling silver sheet for the desired width of the ring. (This ring is 16 mm wide.) Cut out the silver with a saw or step shear.

2. Roll the remaining sterling silver sheet through the rolling mill, thinning it to 22 gauge.

3. Design two leaf shapes to be sweat soldered onto the band of the ring. (Here, the decorative shapes echo the flower petals.) Cut these shapes out of the thinned sterling silver sheet. File and sand the shapes smooth.

4. Mark the center of the 18-gauge silver strip. (Note: When the strip is later bent into a band, this center mark will be at the top of the band. You will want to position the leaf shapes accordingly.) Sweat solder the leaf shapes onto the band, near each side of the marked center point. Pickle the metal.

5. Round the band on a ring mandrel, using a rawhide mallet. Because the strip is longer than a standard ring size, the ends of the band will overlap. Mark the band at the desired ring size, and cut through both layers of the band with a saw. Solder the band closed with hard solder. Round the soldered band on a ring mandrel with a rawhide mallet. Evenly sand and smooth all edges.

6. At the top of the band, between the leaf shapes, drill halfway through the metal with a 1.85 mm bit. (Start with a smaller bit first, then work up to the final size.) This partial hole will hold the tube for the flower stem. (The 1.85 mm bit is slightly larger than the outside diameter of the tubing, which allows for a little solder.)

7. Cut a piece of tubing that is longer than you want the flower stem to be. (This allows for soldering and some trim-

> **"I think it is so important as artists to keep pushing ourselves, in both design and technique, so that we continue to grow and evolve."**

ming.) Sand the cut ends of the tubing, and solder it into the partial hole in the band with hard solder. (If you're worried that the solder on the leaf shapes will reflow, use yellow ochre or some other solder stop.)

8. Design a small leaf shape that is substantial enough to support the weight of a large flower, and cut out the shape from copper sheet. (This is the "foot" of the ring that allows it to stand.) If needed, flatten the shape with a rawhide mallet on a wooden block. Using medium solder, solder this leaf to the bottom of the band ring, opposite the tubing.

Making the Flower Petals

1. Roll the remaining copper sheet in the rolling mill, thinning it to 22 gauge.

2. Design three small and six large petal shapes, and cut them out of the thinned copper sheet. (Use any leaf shape or petal shape found in the garden, or invent a shape. I used real columbine leaves as a pattern for my petal design.) Texture the petals as desired, and then sand their edges. (I used a rough sanding wheel to texture the inside surface of the petals and a piece of 280-grit sandpaper to texture the outside surface.)

Making the Setting for the Stone

1. Select a copper washer with an inside diameter that is slightly smaller than the girdle of your stone. (The stone should sit down inside the washer, but not fall through.) With a 0.91 mm bit, drill four holes on opposite sides of the washer to accommodate the prongs. Cut four 1-inch (2.5 cm) lengths of sterling silver wire. Melt a ball on one end of each wire.

2. Slide one balled wire through each drilled hole in the washer. The wires should be facing the same way, with all the balls sitting on one side of the washer. Hold the washer upside down in cross-locking tweezers with the balls on top, and solder the balled wires into holes in the washer with hard solder.

3. Determine how much wire is needed to prong set your stone (keeping in mind that the ends of the wires will be melted into balls), and cut off any excess. Melt these ends into very slight balls. The washer has been transformed into a seat for your stone, with four balls sitting flush against one side and four balled wires slightly protruding from the other. Use a cup burr to round the ends of the balled wires.

Attaching the Petals & Dome

1. Position the seat for the stone on a soldering block with the protruding wire prongs facing down. Arrange the three small copper petals at regular intervals around the seat. Gently bend the ends of the petals as necessary with your fingers or with pliers to get good contact with the copper washer and to ensure a good solder seam. Solder the small petals to the washer with minimal hard solder. (If solder leaks onto the inside of the petals, it will be seen on the ring.)

2. Following the method described in the step above, position the remaining six larger petals around the copper washer. Solder them in place with hard solder.

3. To make a cup for the underside of the flower, cut a circle out of the 22-gauge copper sheet, and dome it in a dapping block. (I used a circle with a 3.5 cm diameter, but you may need to alter the size of your circle based on the size of your flower. Choose a size that, when domed, will cover all the ends of the flower petals.)

4. Flow hard solder onto the underside of the dome where the petals will touch it. Position the dome upside down over the petal structure and heat the whole piece—petals and dome—until the solder flows and solders the elements.

5. Using a 1.78 mm bit, drill a hole in the top of the dome for the silver tube "stem." Cut the stem to the desired length. Position the flower upside down with the ring band balanced in a pair of cross-locking tweezers, and solder the stem into the hole in the copper dome with medium solder.

6. Inspect the dome and the petals. If there are gaps around the petals where the dome doesn't meet them, gently hammer around the dome with a small ball peen or riveting hammer to bring the dome down slightly against the petals. (The copper will move quickly because it is annealed from soldering.) Texture the dome as desired. (I used a cutoff disk to make vertical marks around the edge of the dome.)

7. If desired, make a subtle bend in the flower stem by gently pulling the flower with your fingers. Do not bend too much or the tube will kink. Give the petals any kind of "gesture" you want by bending their edges and tips.

Finishing the Ring

1. Finish the flower as desired—sand, tumble, or brush. (I tumbled the flower in abrasive media for about an hour, and then tumbled it in steel shot to harden the metal.)

2. Dip the flower into a strong solution of liver of sulfur. Dip and rinse it in cool water several times to build up a deep layer of patina. Do not dip the ring shank or tubing into the liver of sulfur. With a small brush, paint liver of sulfur onto the foot of the ring until black. Rinse and dry the ring thoroughly. Rub the blackened areas with a piece of clean scrub pad to buff, taking off as much or as little of the patina as desired. If desired, spray the ring with a clear lacquer to protect the finish.

3. Place the stone in the seat, and push the prongs over with a bezel pusher.

Insight

In keeping with the challenge aspect of the project, I really wanted to make something that was challenging to me, and I think I succeeded. I think it is so important as artists to keep pushing ourselves, in both design and technique, so that we continue to grow and evolve. Although the organic flower form is one that is familiar in my work, the design I settled on and the techniques I used to bring that design to life really pushed me beyond my comfort zone. Along the way, there were several times I wasn't sure I'd be able to execute the design I had sketched on paper, but in the end, the ring turned out even better than what I had pictured in my mind.

artist: Sarah Hood

Created by **Pauline Warg**

Design Number XXX

hand-cut jump rings
highlight artistry...uses the
mesh like cloisonné wire—
a lovely effect...classic
technique for original look

Tools & Materials

Bench tool kit, page 6
Soldering kit, page 6
Photocopied design template A, page 126
Photocopied design template B, page 126
Straight chasing liner tool
Matting tools
Permanent marker
6 nonleaded opaque enamels
    (medium temperature, medium fusing)
Klyr-fire enamel binder
Distilled water
Paintbrush, 00 sable
Kiln with firing rack and fork
Knife
Alundum stone, 150 and 220 grit
Diamond cloth, 200, 400 and 1800 grit
Glass brush
Polishing compounds, Tripoli and
    red rouge
Unstitched muslin buffing wheels
Polishing machine
Ultrasonic cleaner
Liver of sulfur
Detergent
Ring clamp
Radial bristle disk, 400 grit

Wildcard

Enamel

From the Box

Method

Preparing the Components

1. Anneal the sterling silver sheet. Transfer photocopied template A onto the surface.

2. Secure the silver sheet on a steel bench block with tape or a soft-tipped clamp. Draw the lines to be chased with a fine-tip marker. Use a straight chasing tool and chasing hammer to incise the drawn lines. When the metal becomes hardened and begins to curl up, remove it from the block and reanneal it. Resecure the metal on the bench block, and continue chasing until complete.

3. Hammer matting textures onto all the smooth sections between the chased lines with matting tools. (Chasing and matting may stretch and distort the sheet metal. Retrace the squares, triangle, and rectangle as required.)

4. Carefully saw out the squares, the triangle, and the rectangle just outside the edge of the traced lines. File then sand the edges of each shape until very smooth. Drill a 1 mm hole inside the interior triangle, and then pierce out the interior shape. File the edges of the pierced shape. (This shape will be the opening for the toggle clasp.)

5. Transfer photocopied template B onto the copper sheet. Saw out the individual shapes, then file and sand the cut edges. Pierce and saw out an interior triangle on one of the copper pieces, as shown on the template.

6. Arrange all the silver panels in the desired order. Using a permanent marker, write a number, 1 through 7, on the back of each panel. (The numbers represent the order in which the silver pieces will be assembled.) Rewrite the numbers on the backs of the pieces with a steel scribe. (This way the numbers will not be rubbed off during the construction of the bracelet. The marks can be removed during final finishing.)

"**I wanted to use as many of the items provided and still have the piece be representative of my design sense and the techniques I normally use.**"

7. Measure and mark the back of each silver panel and the toggle clasp to match the template. Drill a 1 mm hole at each mark. Redrill each hole with a 2 mm bit, and clean up any burrs.

8. Measure and mark the back of each copper triangle and the toggle clasp to match the template. Drill a 0.88 mm hole at each mark.

9. Dap all copper and silver pieces (except the rectangular toggle) in the largest recess of a wood dapping block.

10. On the leftover sterling silver sheet, measure 2.4 cm inside the long straight edge, and scribe a line down the length of the piece (see the template on page 126). Trim off the irregular edge with a jeweler's saw. The piece should now be a rectangle that is approximately 2.4 x 5.1 cm.

11. Cut 16 strips from the leftover silver sheet, each 2.4 cm long x 1.6 mm wide. These strips will become the jump rings that connect the bracelet panels. Do not bother sanding the long edge of the strips at this point.

12. Bend the thin silver strips into rings with round or flat forming pliers. Solder the seams of the rings shut with hard silver solder. One by one, place a soldered ring on a round bezel mandrel, and tap with a rawhide mallet until they are round and symmetrical. Then place each ring flat on a piece of 400-grit sandpaper. Move the ring in a circular motion until the sides are smooth and flat.

13. The leftover silver sheet should now measure approximately 2.4 x 1.9 cm. Cut several small strips from the leftover sheet, each 1.6 mm wide x 1.9 cm. Follow step 12 to form these strips into rings. These will be extra rings of a smaller diameter to have on hand.

14. Hold one of the copper triangles over the fine silver mesh. Trim the mesh with shears around the perimeter of the copper, leaving a slight amount of excess around the edges. Repeat this step with the remaining five copper pieces. Dap the screen pieces into the wood dapping block, using the same recess that was used for the silver and copper pieces (step 9).

Enameling the Links

1. Thoroughly clean the copper pieces. Only hold the copper by its edges during and after the cleaning.

2. Choose six colors of dry enamel. (This project features Thompson's nonleaded opaques: 1140, 1150, 1880, 1890, 1920, and 1995—2 browns, 2 reds, gray, and black.) Each enamel color needs a separate ½ oz. (15 mL) jar with a lid. Write the number of the enamel on the lid of the jar with a permanent marker. Put 1 teaspoon of each dry enamel in the appropriate jar. Use an eyedropper to add a 50/50 solution of Klyr-fire binder and distilled water until the enamel is saturated and a thin layer of liquid covers the top.

3. Place one mesh screen on each copper triangle, and arrange the stacks in the order that they will sit on the silver panels.

4. Using a 00 sable paintbrush, gather up a small amount of wet enamel and paint it into the screen over the copper. (Always rinse the brush before using another color. Cross contamination of colors in the jars will ruin your palette.) Continue this process until enamel covers each piece. This will not be smooth and even.

5. Turn on the kiln and set the temperature to 1450°F (788°C). Carefully pick up the copper pieces by the edges or by slipping a knife underneath them, and set them on a firing rack to dry. When the kiln reaches temperature, lift up the firing rack with a firing fork and place it in the kiln. Set a timer for two minutes. When the timer goes off, open the kiln and lift the rack out with a firing fork. Set the rack down on a fireproof surface, and let the pieces air cool.

6. Check the cooled pieces for low spots in the enamel. Add more wet enamel with the brush as needed to fill the low areas, and let dry. Refire the pieces for two minutes. Repeat this step until the enamel is covering or level with the top of the screen. If there are high spots covering the screen, don't be concerned at this point.

7. Using metal shears, trim off the extra screen from the edges of the enameled copper pieces. If the enamel seems to have filled in all of the mesh, it's time to start grinding the surface flush. Under running water, grind the enameled surface with an alundum stone or diamond cloth until the surface seems flatter and the grid of the screen is revealed. Dry and inspect the piece. The surface will be dull where it has been abraded. Shiny spots on the surface indicate a lack of enamel. Add more enamel to these areas, refire, cool, and grind the piece.

8. Trim the mesh on the inside of the toggle shape with a jeweler's saw or fine-tipped metal shears. Grind the edges of each enameled shape to make the screen, enamel, and copper even and smooth. Do a final grinding, ending with 1800-grit on the edges and top enameled surfaces. Scrub the pieces with a glass brush, and rinse them with water.

9. One at a time, place the enameled pieces in a shallow jar cap or lid covered with water, and redrill the holes in the enameled pieces from the back with a 20-gauge diamond drill bit. Fire the pieces one more time to create a fire polish on the enamel.

Assembling the Base of the Bracelet

1. Cut 18 pieces of sterling wire, each 1.4 cm long. Use a torch to melt a small ball at the end of each wire piece. Pickle, rinse, and dry the wires, then put them aside. Adjust a tube-cutting jig to 1.5 mm. Saw 18 pieces of the silver tubing, each 2 mm long. Sand the cut edges smooth.

2. One by one, center each enameled piece onto the corresponding silver panel. Hold the enameled piece firmly in place while drilling through the enameled piece and then the silver piece with a 20-gauge bit in the flex shaft. (This is the first rivet

hole.) Repeat this process for the remaining two holes. Continue this process until three rivet holes are drilled in each silver panel. When the drilling is complete, set the enameled pieces aside.

Expert Tip: Placing a balled wire into the first set of holes will help keep the pieces lined up when drilling the second and third hole.

---

3. Slice through the solder seam on each of the larger jump rings. Open them with pliers, and use them to connect all the silver panels and toggle catch in numerical order. (The two rings on the end of the sixth panel will become the attachment to the toggle bar.) Solder each of the 12 rings shut with medium solder.

4. Saw a 1.3 x 3.2 cm rectangle out of the copper sheet. Sweat solder the silver toggle rectangle to the copper rectangle with hard solder. Saw off the excess copper from around the edges of the sterling toggle. File and sand the edges even and smooth.

5. Saw a 0.16 x 1.6 cm strip from the leftover 18-gauge sterling sheet. Shape this thin strip into a jump ring with round or flat forming pliers. Position this jump ring on edge across the center of the copper side of the toggle bar, and solder it in place with medium solder.

6. At the end of the sixth silver panel, link three of the small jump rings in a chain. The first small ring links through the large rings on the end of the panel, and the third jump ring connects to the toggle bar. Solder the links closed with medium solder.

Finishing All the Components

1. Remove the scribed numbers on the back of each silver panel with a medium rubber wheel on the flex shaft. Buff the assembled silver bracelet thoroughly with Tripoli compound and an un-stitched muslin buff on a polishing machine. (No need to buff the front, textured side at this point. Concentrate on the soldered rings and backs of the panels.) Clean the bracelet in an ultrasonic cleaner.

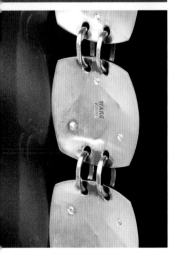

2. Oxidize the silver bracelet in a liver of sulfur solution. When the bracelet is completely blackened, remove it from the solution with copper tongs and rinse thoroughly with water.

3. Buff the entire silver bracelet using red rouge compound on a muslin buff. (This removes the oxidation from the high spots and backs of the panels.) Clean the bracelet in an ultrasonic cleaner. Rinse and dry it.

4. Carefully buff the enameled pieces with red rouge compound to shine the mesh. Wash the rouge off by using a drop of detergent and gently rubbing the enameled pieces with thumb and index finger. Rinse well and pat dry with a soft cloth.

5. Place the melted wires in the flat end of a ring clamp with their balled ends exposed. Buff the balls with red rouge, then wash and dry them.

Attaching the Enameled Triangles

1. One panel at a time, gather three of the wires with melted ends, three pieces of 1.5 mm x 1.5 mm tubing, the matching number enameled piece and silver panel, and prepare the assembly for riveting. Feed the wire through the enameled piece with the balled end on top. Slide the tubing onto the other, unmelted wire end (on the backside of the enamel). Set up all three of the wires to this point.

2. Guide the wires, with the tubing on them, into the holes on the front side of the silver panel. Rest the enameled panel, with wires and tubing through it, facedown on a steel bench block. Clip the wires approximately 0.5 mm from the back surface of the silver panel. One by one, rivet the clipped wires, forming a small mushroom head over the hole. Repeat this process until all six panels are riveted. Put a satin finish on the back of the bracelet with a 400-grit radial bristle disk.

Insight

When I first got the challenge invitation I didn't hesitate; I replied, "I'm game." I'm always up for a good challenge. As soon as I had the written descriptions of the materials, I started designing in my mind. I tend to suffer from performance anxiety and wanted to make sure I'd be ready when everything arrived. Due to my on-the-road teaching schedule and some custom orders, my biggest challenge was finding enough bench time to actually get my piece made in the designated time. I wanted to use as many of the items provided and still have the piece be representative of my design sense and the techniques I normally use. I gravitated to creating a bracelet using enamel as my wildcard. The shapes in the bracelet are the shapes I use most frequently, and the techniques of chasing, matting, and enameling are three of my most favorite techniques. I made a few prototypes of the enameled panels to hone in on a palette. All went according to plan, and I felt comfortable and enjoyed the process.

artist: Pauline Warg

About the Artists

Boris Bally's award-winning work is both witty and innovative, employing the use of jewelers' skills on non-precious materials. His current body of work transforms recycled street signs, weapon parts, and a wide variety of found materials into objects for reflection. These pieces celebrate a raw American street aesthetic in the form of objects, often useful, for the home and the body. Boris is the recipient of the 2006 Individual Achievement Award for the Visual Arts, presented by the Arts & Business Council of Rhode Island. He is a past recipient of two Rhode Island Council on the Arts Fellowships in Design and one Pennsylvania Council on the Arts Fellowship in Craft. His work

is featured in numerous international exhibitions and publications. Public collections include London's V&A Museum, Museum of Art & Design, Carnegie Museum of Art, Brooklyn Museum, Renwick Gallery, and Cooper Hewitt National Design Museum.

Colleen Baran is a Canadian jeweler who has exhibited in galleries and museums in 11 countries and has been published in a couple more. In 2008, she had her first solo show—Like Wearing a Love Letter—at the Crafthouse Gallery in Vancouver, Canada. Since 2006, Colleen's work has been featured in 9 books including: *The Art and Craft of Making Jewelry* by Joanna Gollberg, *Chain Mail Jewelry* by Terry Taylor, *500 Wedding Rings* edited by Marthe Le Van, *500 Plastic Jewelry* also edited by Marthe Le Van (all Lark Books), and *The Jeweler's Studio Handbook* by Brandon Holschuh.

Davide Bigazzi's handcrafted jewelry and hollowware are a blend of contemporary artistry and old world craftsmanship that echo back to his native Florence, Italy. Capturing the intrinsic beauty and sculptural qualities of precious metals has been his lifelong passion. Davide is renowned for his mastery of chasing and repoussè, the ancient art of shaping and embellishing metal with raised bas-relief designs. From a young age, he apprenticed under one of the last remaining Italian masters of this highly expressive art form, Bino Bini. At the age of 19,

Davide began to pursue his own career, first as a bench jeweler, then as designer, model maker, and production supervisor for commercial manufacturers. In 1995, Davide received the International Artisans Award given during the international exhibition *Mostra Internazionale dell' Artigianato*. The honor spurred him to quit his design career and return to handcrafting one piece at a time. Today, Davide and his wife Elisa run the Davide Bigazzi Studio and Gallery in Menlo Park, California. Davide currently exhibits in

art shows and fine galleries throughout the country and abroad, and teaches chasing and repoussè in the U.S. and Italy.

Annie Chau studied jewelry and metalsmithing at Towson University in Baltimore, Maryland, where she now resides. Her work can be found in boutiques and galleries around the globe. When Annie is not at the bench, you can find her on the yoga mat, in the kitchen concocting vegan meals, or cycling around her fair city.

Ross Coppelman has been designing and hand-fabricating jewelry on Cape Cod for nearly 40 years. Primarily self-taught, he was first shown the "blobbing" technique by Bernard Kelly in the early 1970s, but hadn't used it for 35 years, until now. He maintains a showroom and workshop year-round in East Dennis, MA. His work can be seen at www.coppelman.com.

Candie Cooper is a jewelry designer with a passion for combining unique materials and colors, inspired by extensive travel and her years living in China. Candie is the author of *Felted Jewelry* and *Designer Needle Felting* (both Lark Books, 2007) and is a contributing designer in Lark's *Fabulous Found Object Jewelry*, *Beading with Crystals*, and *Beading with Charms*. Currently she's creating designs for a variety of companies in the craft industry as well as for craft and jewelry-making publications. Candie teaches workshops both nationally and internationally

and has appeared on the Public Television series *Beads, Baubles, and Jewels*. She earned a Bachelor's degree in Art Education and Fine Arts from Purdue University. For further information, please visit www.candiecooper.com.

Robert Dancik holds a master's degree in sculpture from Northern Illinois University and a B.F.A. from Adelphi University. He has been an artist and teacher for more than 30 years, and is presently an adjunct professor of education at Pace University. Robert has taught people from kindergarten to graduate school, while exhibiting his jewelry and sculpture in museums and galleries across the U.S. and in Europe, Japan, and Australia. His work is featured in many books, such as *500 Pendants, 1000 Rings, The*

Art of Resin Jewelry, and *Creative Metal Clay Jewelry*. His writing and artwork have appeared in magazines like *Niche*, *Art Jewelry*, and *Lapidary Journal*. Robert is the originator of Faux Bone™, a new material for artists involved in jewelry, artist's books, sculpture, and many other artistic disciplines. His book, *Amulets and Talismans: Techniques for Making Meaningful Jewelry*, will be available in June of 2009. Robert lives in Lostwithiel, Cornwall, UK, where he teaches, is an avid cook (though he doesn't claim to be good), and a collector of toys, maps, and compasses. See more of Robert's work at www.robertdancik.com.

In September 2007, **Jennaca Davies** launched her own design company, Jennaca Davies Studio. She received her master's degree from the Rhode Island School of Design in 2007; and since graduation has continued her exploration with new technologies such as laser cutting, waterjet cutting, and CAD CAM. She also employs traditional metalsmithing techniques such as enameling and fabrication. Jennaca's work had been exhibited at the Talente 2007 exhibition as part of the International Handwerksmesse in Munich, Germany. She has received numerous awards, including the Hayward Prize for Fine Arts from the American Austrian Foundation, the MJSA Scholarship in 2005 and 2006 through the Rhode Island Foundation, and recently spent a semester as an artist in residence at the Oregon College of Art and Craft. Jennaca received bach-

elor's of architecture and bachelor's of building science degrees from Rensselaer Polytechnic Institute and continues to practice architecture part time.

Born in 1938 in Topeka, Kansas, **Bob Ebendorf** received his B.F.A. in 1960 and his M.F.A. in 1962. Following graduation, he received a Fulbright Fellowship to study at the State School of Applied Arts in Norway. He has taught at the University of Georgia and at the State University of New York at New Paltz. In 1995, he was awarded the American Craft Council Fellowship for his achievement in crafts and his commitment to the craft movement. Bob is co-founder and past president of the Society of North American Goldsmiths (SNAG) and is represented in many worldwide collections, including the Metropolitan Museum of New York; the Victoria and Albert Museum (England); the Museum of Fine Arts in Boston; the Mint Museum of Craft Design in Charlotte, North Carolina; Le Musee des Arts Decoratifs de Montreal; and the National Museum of Wales, to name a few. He currently serves as the Belk Distinguished Professor in Art at East Carolina University in Greenville, North Carolina.

Kathy Frey is a full-time studio jeweler. Her line of handcrafted sculptural wire jewelry shows a distinctive flair, influenced by her graphic design background. The work features

linear details, contrast, and interesting use of negative space and form. More than 60 galleries, boutiques, and museum shops carry her jewelry, and she also represents her own work at many fine art fairs. Outside the studio, you can find Kathy rock climbing at the gym, cooking, or sipping a glass of wine while watching an action movie.

After receiving her B.A. in Humanities, **Joanna Gollberg** attended the Fashion Institute of Technology in NYC and earned an A.A.S. degree in Jewelry Design in 1997. Now she is a full-time studio jeweler in Asheville, NC. She has also written four books on making jewelry and home items out of metal: *Making Metal Jewelry*, *Creative Metal Crafts*, *The Art and Craft of Making Jewelry*, and *The Jeweler's Guide: An Illustrated Reference of Techniques, Tools, & Materials*, all published by Lark Books. She is a frequent contributor to many other

Lark Books and does freelance how-to writing for the *Lapidary Journal* and *Art Jewelry Magazine*. She also teaches jewelry making at the John C. Campbell Folk School, Penland School of Crafts, and Arrowmont School of Crafts. She sells her work at craft fairs and galleries throughout the U.S.

Rebecca Hannon graduated from Rhode Island School of Design and then worked as a goldsmith for five years in New York City, before attending the Akademie der Bildenden Kuenste in Munich, Germany, on a Fulbright Scholarship. Five years later, she returned to the states and currently teaches, lectures, and has her own workshop in Ithaca, NY. Her work can be found in public and private collections internationally.

Mary Hettmansperger is a fiber and jewelry artist who exhibits and teaches across the U.S. and abroad. Arrowmont School of Crafts, Bead and Button Conference, Convergence, national conferences, guilds, and similar venues are some of the places she lends her instruction

on jewelry, basketry, surface design, and quilting. Mary's artwork is represented at SOFA–Chicago by the Katie Gingrass gallery.

She has authored and illustrated two books on jewelry, *Fabulous Woven Jewelry*, and *Wrap, Stitch, Fold, and Rivet*, both published by Lark Books. A third jewelry book on mixed metals will be released from Lark in the spring of 2010. Her work can also be found in *500 Baskets, Fiber Arts Design Book 7, Fabulous Found Object Jewelry, Teapots—Makers/Collectors, Beading with Crystals*, and others. Television segments include the PBS programs "Beads, Baubles, and Jewels" and "Quilting Art." She has also published work in numerous magazines.

Many years ago, **Sarah Hood** found herself sitting in a beginning jewelry making course at a small California college, and from that moment on, she was hooked. She went on to formalize her studies at Parsons School of Design in New York City, while simultaneously earning a writing degree from The New School. After earning her B.A., she finished a B.F.A. in metalsmithing at the University of Washington in Seattle.  She currently lives and works in Seattle, and has been an active member of the lively arts community there for many years.

Makers run in **Deb Karash's** family. Her grandfather was  a tool and die maker and a toy designer, her father a woodworker, and her mother has always sewn, knitted, and crocheted. Even as a child, rather than play with dolls, Deb made things for them. She came to jewelry making in her late 20s, and it was then that she felt she had found her life's passion, though it wouldn't be until the age of 40 that she would make it her vocation, becoming a full-time studio jeweler. Soon after that, she began drawing on metal, and that technique has held her interest ever since. Soon after, teaching brought her to the mountains of North Carolina, and she decided to make them her home. Now she spends most of her time in her studio, which is a renovated high school on a small island in the middle of the French Broad River in a small town in the Blue Ridge Mountains. Deb spends her free time working to bring sustainable economic development to her town, and enjoying the natural beauty of Western North Carolina. Marshall High Studios is home not only to her studio, but also to those of many talented people who provide a constant source of inspiration and community.

Kristin Lora has been creating jewelry and sculptural objects for over 30 years. Although her formal education is in Zoology and Business, Kristin is both self-taught and has studied metal techniques in various institutions over the years. Kristin's work has been featured in numerous books and maga-

zines (such as Lark Book's *500 Pendants and Lockets* and *Mixed Media Jewelry*) as well as being featured on HGTV. Her work is represented by over 40 galleries across the U.S. Kristin's jewelry is known for its clean, uncomplicated, and contemporary lines, and is inspired by observations of everyday life occurrences, collected objects, and an unconventional imagination.

Sydney Lynch has always liked making things. The process of transforming raw materials into something beautiful is gratifying and magical. And she particularly loves it when people find their own meanings in her designs. Sydney's work is both sculptural and contemporary with references to natural forms, creating an  organic geometry in which shapes are juxtaposed to achieve a sense of balance and proportion. Comfort and wearability are primary concerns in her designs. She finds design potential everywhere: in natural forms, landscapes, weathered cityscapes, visits to art museums. All of these experiences are combined and translated intuitively into jewelry designs. See more of Sydney's work at www.sydneylynch.com.

Marcia Macdonald has a B.F.A. in Design from the University of North Carolina at Greensboro and an M.F.A. in Jewelry and Metals from the University of Massachusetts at Dartmouth. Owner of Macdonald Designs, Marcia says her business has many facets. She divides her time between designing and making one-of-a-kind jewelry and limited edition production pieces and teaching classes in design and fabrication of jewelry. She also has a home organizing business called WHISK Home Organizing. Her work has been shown at craft shows such as the Smithsonian Museum of Art Craft show, the Philadelphia Museum of Art Craft show, and the American Craft Council shows. Marcia is a past board member for the Society of North American Goldsmiths and has exhibited both nationally and internationally. She has  been published in numerous books, and has taught workshops at Penland School of Crafts, Arrowmont School of Crafts, Haystack Mountain School of Crafts, and at numerous university art programs. She is an award-winning, professional artist who has a passion for designing, making, and organizing.

Chihiro Makio has always loved creating precious little things, even from an early age. While in college for a studio art major, she discovered the endless possibilities with three-dimensional materials, working with wood, fiber, metal, and eventually

glass. She completed a B.F.A. at the Massachusetts College of Art as a glass major with a minor in small metals/jewelry. Chihiro continued to work on her jewelry after graduating in 2000, and started a small business in 2002. She received second place in the silver category for the Saul Bell Design Award in 2005. She also won the 2005 and 2008 Niche Awards for the "Sculpture to Wear" category. Her work can be seen at select craft galleries and museum shops throughout the country, including the Aaron Faber Gallery in New York and the Luke and Eloy Gallery in Pittsburgh, Pennsylvania.

Thomas Mann is best known for his Techno.Romantic Jewelry Objects™. Originally from Pennsylvania, Tom exhibited his work at The New Orleans Jazz and Heritage Festival in 1977 and

has called New Orleans home ever since. However, it would be more accurate to call the United States at-large his home, since he spends most of his time on the road exhibiting at as many as 15 nationally juried craft and art events each year, in addition to teaching workshops and public speaking. Somehow, he still finds time to oversee the management and art direction of a jewelry studio and gallery. Over the last few years, he has moved away from his signature Techno.Romantic design vocabulary toward jewelry designs that are models for large-scale sculpture. You can see Tom's work at www.thomasmann.com. His studio in New Orleans is open for visits and tours.

Tim McCreight is a metalsmith, designer, author, and teacher. He has been working in metals since 1970 and along the way has published two dozen books and made six videos. He is a former president of the Society of North American Goldsmiths (SNAG), and has served on the boards of Haystack, the American Craft Council, and the PMC Guild. Tim has taught workshops in the U.S., England, Canada, Mexico, Norway, and Japan. He writes for several magazines and runs a publishing company in Maine called Brynmorgen Press.

Danielle Miller-Gilliam grew up in a steel mill town in the Laurel Highlands of western Pennsylvania. Being surrounded by beautiful rolling hills juxtaposed by bridges, railroads, and

industry greatly influenced her design sensibility. Her work is geometric, often mechanical, and uses natural influences that are stripped down to their core shapes. Danielle discovered her passion for metals while making a large-scale welded steel sculpture as a high school student. She

studied at the Tyler School of Art at Temple University, where she received a bachelor's degree in fine art, concentrating on Jewelry and Metals. After college, she gained invaluable experience perfecting her skills by working under a master goldsmith. In 1995, she participated in her first craft show, and by 1998 was able to devote herself full-time to her own business. Today, Danielle's jewelry designs can be seen in galleries throughout the country. She now makes her home in the foothills of the Blue Ridge Mountains in South Carolina with her husband, Ben Gilliam, and their two sons.

Over the past 28 years, the content in **Tod Pardon's** work, both in metals and video, has been influenced by elements that are vast, varied, and personal. He sees his work as an expression of life's inherent duality and instability. There are contradictions of anxiety and humor, good and evil. The humor and color play an important role in contrast to the sometimes screaming pieces—much like the Balinese Barong dance of good versus evil. The character he is drawn to most is Rangda, Queen of the

Leyaks. She is a bloodthirsty, child-eating, witching-widow mistress of black magic, and is feared and nasty, but is portrayed and acts in a comical way. It's like you can't see the light without the dark. Or, as Rabindranath Tagore, the well-known poet from India, says, "truth in her dress finds facts too tight, in fiction she moves with ease."

A self-taught goldsmith and jeweler, **Todd Reed** recalls that his affinity for jewelry making started around the age of 10 while on a family vacation in Bisbee, Arizona. After designing furniture, clothes, sculpting, painting, and graduating with honors

from culinary school, Todd officially launched a jewelry collection under his own name in 1992 and set out to change jewelry's future by creating solely with raw and uncut diamonds. His work has been featured in many of the finest books on goldsmithing and art jewelry. He has received multiple awards—such as the Town & Country Couture Award in 2008—and has been honored by the American Craft Council and the Society of North American Goldsmiths. For the past two years, Todd has served as the president on the board of The American Jewelry Design Council.

Janette Schuster is a freelance writer, artist, workshop instructor, and incurable treasure hunter. Formally trained as a geologist and archaeologist, she has been digging up artifacts all her life. Janette now indulges her love of found relics, modern to ancient, by using them in jewelry, collage, assemblage, and mosaics. Her work has appeared in many publications, and she is the author of *Mixed-Media Collage Jewelry: New Directions in Memory Jewelry* (Lark Books, 2009). Her work is available through her art website at www.VisualApothecary.com.

Biba Schutz is a self-taught, fine-art-educated maker of jewelry. Having spent twenty plus years as a jeweler in New York City exploring and developing her voice, Biba consistently stretches boundaries and challenges her own ideas and skills. Her jewelry and objects bring mystery and association to the

visual and tactile senses. Front, interior, and back surfaces interact, drawing the eye and memories into a drama of hidden places. Exploring form, line, space, and texture, BIba encourages visual and emotional exploration. Though it may look spontaneous, her work carefully calculated to create movement, space, rhythm, and shadow. Biba draws inspiration from her environment, botanicals, archaeology, and the mundane.

Eric Silva's jewelry is a handmade collection of wearable sculpture made with eco-conscious materials such as rustic sterling silver, shed deer antler, recycled wood, and semi-precious stones. Based in Whittier, California, Eric's garage has been the workshop of his many artistic creations.

His work has been featured in several magazines garnered him number awards, including the Exhibitor's Choice Silver Award at the 2008 Smithsonian Craft Show and the Jewelry Award of Excellence and Originality at the 2008 Ann Arbor Street Fair, the Original. Eric has devoted himself to his work, supporting his family, which includes 4 boys, all home-schooled, and traveling across the country to about a dozen shows a year while putting on exhibitions and having time to hold workshops. In his spare time, Eric enjoys surfing, cooking, and Bikram yoga. To see more of Eric's work, visit www.ericsilva.com.

Marlene True works as a studio artist in the Richmond, Virginia, area. She earned her B.F.A. from Southern Illinois University in Edwardsville and an M.F.A. from East Carolina University, both in Jewelry and Metal. Her work has evolved from creating jewelry and objects with traditional materials to a passion for using re-

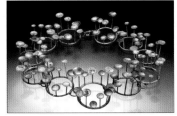

claimed tin, both as a design element and material for fabrication. Marlene's work has been widely exhibited and can be found in many books and private collections. Activities outside the studio include teaching and lecturing at art centers, universities, and organizations, including Arrowmont School of Arts and Crafts, Penland School of Crafts, Society for Midwest Metalsmiths, and Craft Alliance in St. Louis.

Pauline Warg is a metalsmith with 34 years of experience. She earned a Journeyman Metalsmithing Certificate after completing a three-year apprenticeship to Master Goldsmith Philip Morton, and holds a bachelor's of fine art from the University of Southern Maine. Her work ranges from fabricated jewelry making and silversmithing, to enameling both jewelry and hollowware. Currently Pauline owns and operates WARG Enamel and Tool

Center, in Scarborough, Maine. The center features a gallery of her own work, a full service tool and supply store for jewelers and enamelists, and a teaching studio for metalsmithing and enameling. She is the author of *Making Metal Beads* (Lark Books, 2006), and teaches at the Maine College of Art and a variety of other art centers and colleges across the country.

Sara Westermark lives in Wilmington, North Carolina, where she draws inspiration from nature and experiments with design, color, and texture. Her father was an artist, who taught her by example that she could learn to do anything. Primarily a self-taught metalsmith, she has also studied with bench jeweler Gary Pack. Sara feels that her work graphically represents her life, and feels drawn to the permanence of metal. Her formal academic training is in music from

the University of Missouri-Columbia, where she holds a master's degree in music in voice performance. Throughout the day she divides her time between making jewelry and teaching voice lessons. Sara has worked exclusively in metal for the past four years and has read every textbook on metalsmithing that she could find. Currently, Sara shows her work at Port City Pottery & Fine Crafts, and Blue Moon Gift Shops, Wilmington, North Carolina. In addition to selling at regional trade shows, she also sells her work on Etsy (a website for buying and selling handmade objects) and has been one of Etsy's Featured Sellers. Sara is a member of SNAG, Etsy Metal Team, and NATS (National Association of Teachers of Singing).

Templates

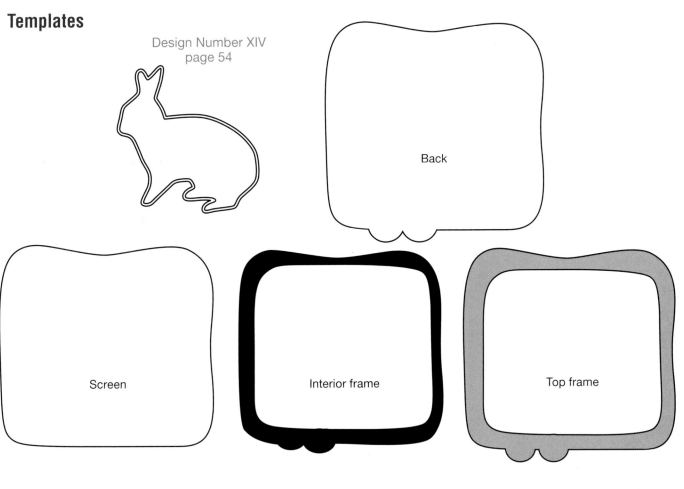

Design Number XIV
page 54

Back

Screen

Interior frame

Top frame

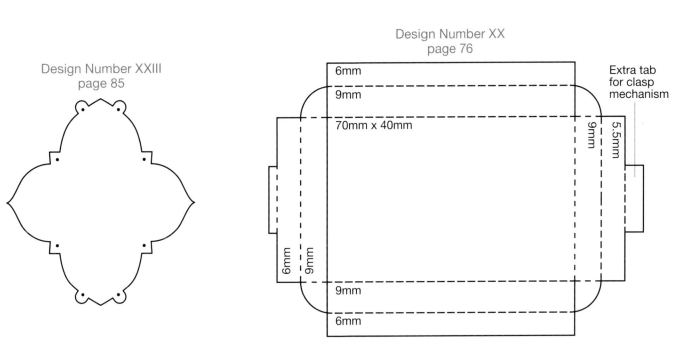

Design Number XXIII
page 85

Design Number XX
page 76

6mm

9mm

70mm x 40mm

9mm

5.5mm

Extra tab
for clasp
mechanism

6mm

9mm

9mm

6mm

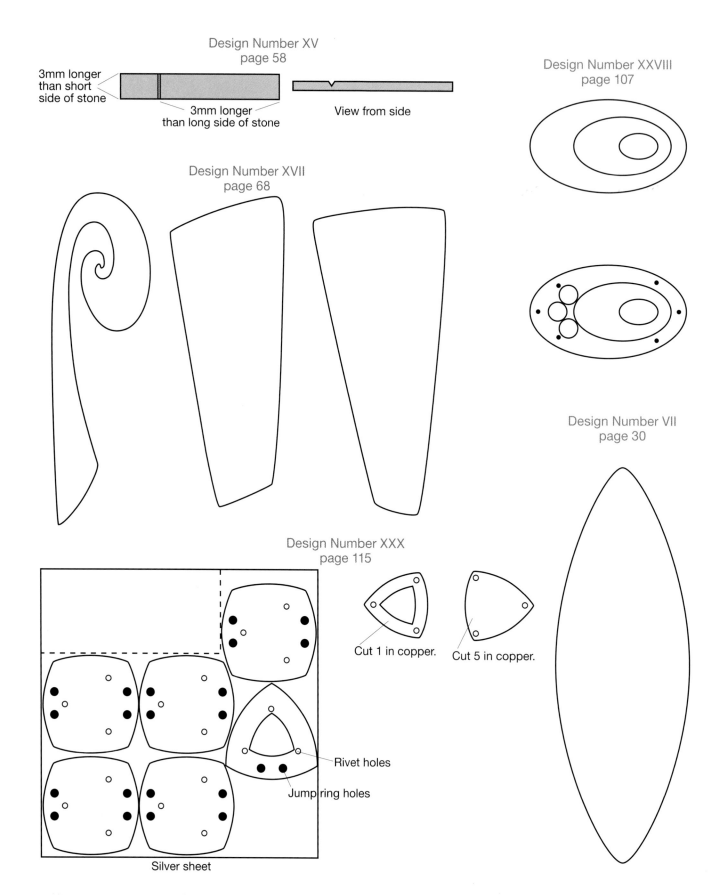

Design Number XV
page 58

3mm longer
than short
side of stone

3mm longer
than long side of stone

View from side

Design Number XXVIII
page 107

Design Number XVII
page 68

Design Number VII
page 30

Design Number XXX
page 115

Cut 1 in copper.

Cut 5 in copper.

Rivet holes

Jump ring holes

Silver sheet

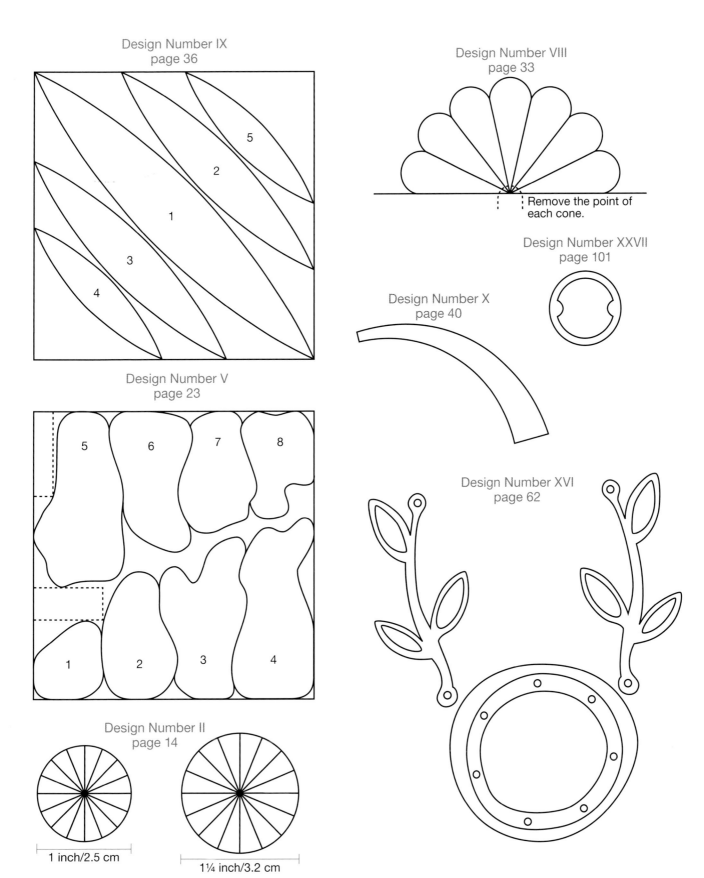

Design Number IX
page 36

Design Number VIII
page 33

Remove the point of
each cone.

Design Number XXVII
page 101

Design Number X
page 40

Design Number V
page 23

Design Number XVI
page 62

Design Number II
page 14

1 inch/2.5 cm

1¼ inch/3.2 cm

Acknowledgments

This book involved a compilation of visions to come to fruition. A lot of thanks go to a lot of people—first and foremost to the incredibly talented artists whose fantastic designs are featured. Amanda Carestio deserves a standing ovation for her unflagging enthusiasm, spot-on suggestions, and unfathomable attention to detail. Accolades and a big high five to all the creative folk who shaped and molded this book… Kathy Holmes, Dana Irwin, Carol Morse, Celia Naranjo, and Stewart O'Shields. Finally, the technical proficiency award goes to Lark's resident jewelry authority, Marthe Le Van. And she's quite the moral supporter, too.

Photographer Index

Boris Bally
Artist image, page 19: J.W. Johnson Photography
Additional artist imagery, page 120: J.W. Johnson Photography

Colleen Baran
Artist image, page 75: Ian McGuffie
Additional artist imagery, page 120: Photos by artist

Davide Bigazzi
Artist image, page 29: Chris Schmauch
Additional artist imagery, page 120: Hap Sakwa

Annie Chau
Artist image, page 67: Stephen Goodman
Additional artist imagery, page 120: Photo by artist

Ross Coppelman
Artist image, page 61: Shannon Mullin
Additional artist imagery, page 120: Ben Coppelman

Candie Cooper
Artist image, page 65: Susan Stewart
Additional artist imagery, page 120: Susan Stewart

Robert Dancik
Artist image, page 44: Douglas Foulke
Additional artist imagery, page 120: Paul Mounsey Photography

Jennaca Davies
Artist image, page 16: Katja Kulenkampff
Additional artist imagery, page 121: Photo by artist

Bob Ebendorf
Artist image, page 47: Forrest Croce
Additional artist imagery, page 121: Marlene True

Kathy Frey
Artist image, page 22: Thea Dickman
Additional artist imagery, page 121: Larry Sanders

Joanna Gollberg
Artist image, page 110: Jamie Stirling
Additional artist imagery, page 121: Photos by artist

Photographer Index cont.

Rebecca Hannon
Artist image, page 35: Anton Christiansen
Additional artist imagery, page 121: Photos by artist

Mary Hettmansperger
Artist image, page 50: Logan Hettmansperger
Additional artist imagery, page 121: Tom Van Eynde

Sarah Hood
Artist image, page 114: John Martin
Additional artist imagery, page 122: Doug Yaple

Deb Karash
Artist image, page 71: Frank Bott
Additional artist imagery, page 122: Larry Sanders

Kristin Lora
Artist image, page 100: Sara Stathas
Additional artist imagery, page 122: Photo by artist

Sydney Lynch
Artist image, page 13: Alan Jackson
Additional artist imagery, page 122: Alan Jackson

Marcia Macdonald
Additional artist imagery, page 122: Hap Sakwa

Chihiro Makio
Additional artist imagery, page 122:
Ivo M. Vermeulen

Thomas Mann
Artist image, page 32: Courtesy of Thomas Mann Design
Additional artist imagery, page 123: Will Crocker (upper), Ralph Gabriner (lower)

Tim McCreight
Artist image, page 81: Mark Blumenthal
Additional artist imagery, page 123: Robert Diamante

Danielle Miller-Gilliam
Artist image, page 39: John B. Gilliam
Additional artist imagery, page 123: Robert Diamante

Tod Pardon
Artist image, page 97: Photo by artist
Additional artist imagery, page 123: Photos by artist

Todd Reed
Artist image, page 84: Cheryl Ungar
Additional artist imagery, page 123: Craig Pratt

Janette Schuster
Additional artist imagery, page 123: Rick Matthews (left), Judith Stalus (right)

Biba Schutz
Artist image, page 77: Ron Boszko
Additional artist imagery, page 124: Ron Boszko

Eric Silva
Artist image, page 93: Denise Silva
Additional artist imagery, page 124: Scott Winslow

Marlene True
Artist image, page 57: Bruce Barnett
Additional artist imagery, page 124: Ralph Gabriner (In the Collection of Clemmer and David Montague)

Pauline Warg
Artist image, page 119: Gary Snider
Additional artist imagery, page 124: Tim Byrne

Sara Westermark
Artist image, page 26: Hans Westermark
Additional artist imagery, page 124: Photos by artist